T0049342

Queen
Goneril

Also by Erin Shields

Queen Goneril

ERIN SHIELDS

Playwrights Canada Press
TORONTO

Playwrights Canada Press
202-269 Richmond St. w., Toronto, ON M5V 1X1
416.703.0013 | info@playwrightscanada.com | www.playwrightscanada.com

LIBRARY AND ARCHIVES CANADA CATALOGUING IN PUBLICATION
Title: Queen Goneril / Erin Shields.
Names: Shields, Erin, author.
Description: A play.
Identifiers: Canadiana (print) 20230465242 | Canadiana (ebook) 20230465250
 | ISBN 9780369104526 (softcover) | ISBN 9780369104533 (PDF)
 | ISBN 9780369104540 (EPUB)
Classification: LCC PS8637.H497 Q44 2023 | DDC c812/.6—dc23

Playwrights Canada Press operates on land which is the current and ancestral home of the Anishinaabe Nations (Ojibwe / Chippewa, Odawa, Potawatomi, Algonquin, Saulteaux, Nipissing, and Mississauga), the Wendat, and the members of the Haudenosaunee Confederacy (Mohawk, Oneida, Onondaga, Cayuga, Seneca, and Tuscarora), as well as Metis and Inuit peoples. It always was and always will be Indigenous land.

We acknowledge the financial support of the Canada Council for the Arts, the Ontario Arts Council (OAC), Ontario Creates, and the Government of Canada for our publishing activities.

For those who are caught in the storm.

Queen Goneril was commissioned by Soulpepper Theatre Company, Toronto, under Artistic Director Weyni Mengesha and Executive Directors Emma Stenning and Gideon Arthurs. It was first produced by Soulpepper in the Marilyn and Charles Baillie Theatre from August 31 through October 2, 2022, in rep with Shakespeare's *King Lear* with the following cast and creative team:

Goneril: Virgilia Griffith
Lear: Tom McCamus
Regan: Vanessa Sears
Cordelia: Helen Belay
Olena/Oswald: Breton Lalama
Old Woman: Nancy Palk
Edmund: Jonathon Young
Gloucester: Oliver Dennis
Kent: Sheldon Elter
Albany: Jordan Pettle
Cornwall: Philip Riccio
Edgar: Damien Atkins

Director: Weyni Mengesha
Assistant Director: Aria Evans
Dramaturge: Guillermo Verdecchia
Assistant Dramaturge: Caitie Graham
Set Designer: Ken MacKenzie
Costume Designer: Judith Bowden
Lighting Designer: Kimberly Purtell
Assistant Lighting Designer: Kara Pankiw
Sound Designer: Thomas Ryder Payne
Fight Director: John Stead
Intimacy Coordinator: Aria Evans
Stage Manager: Robert Harding
Assistant Stage Manager: Kat Chin
Assistant Stage Manager: Farnoosh Talebpour

A Note On The Play

Queen Goneril is set seven years before Shakespeare's play, *King Lear*. The action takes place in and around Lear's palace. Although the play is in relationship to *King Lear*, the characters and story need not be yoked to that narrative. This play is a new play. A play as concerned with what is relevant in our world now as what was relevant in Shakespeare's day. Saying that, it is very interesting for *Queen Goneril* to be performed in rep with *King Lear* as it was in the premiere.

A Note On Casting

This text was written and developed with three Black actresses in mind to play Goneril, Regan, and Cordelia. Alternative casting may be possible, but the three sisters should be from a similar, non-white background. Please consult the playwright to adjust the text accordingly. Lear and Gloucester should be played by white actors. Oswald/Olena should be played by a trans or non-binary actor. As for the rest, you decide.

A Note On Cast Size

A nine-person version of the play is available in which Edgar, Albany, and Cornwall do not appear.

Digital Prologue

The prologue is pre-filmed and played right before the show. It is in the style of a promotional video made by the company rehearsing *King Lear*. The actors playing Lear and Goneril are mid-interview.

The actors are friendly and generous with one another. Performances should be as realistic as possible.

Characters

Goneril (twenty-five, f/cis): strong-willed, independent, intelligent; daughter of Lear, sister to Regan and Cordelia

Regan (twenty-three, f/cis): strong, witty, sexually empowered; daughter of Lear, sister to Goneril and Cordelia

Cordelia (fifteen, f/cis): intelligent, pleasant-seeming, musician; daughter of Lear, sister to Goneril and Regan

Olena/Oswald (mid-twenties, afab/trans person): intelligent, strong, loyal; Goneril's lover

Old Woman (very old, f/cis): clever, scheming, mischievous; future Fool for King Lear

King Lear (seventies, m/cis): doting father, quick to anger, inspired leader somewhat past his prime; father to Goneril, Regan, and Cordelia

Earl of Kent (forties, m/cis): practical, loyal, jovial; general of Lear's army

Earl of Gloucester (sixties, m/cis): scholarly, wine connoisseur; advisor to the king, father to Edmund and Edgar

Edmund (mid-twenties, m/cis): kind, generous, dignified; bastard son of Gloucester, half-brother to Edgar

Edgar (late-twenties, m/cis): son of Gloucester, half-brother to Edmund

Duke of Albany (forties, m/cis): Goneril's husband

Duke of Cornwall (thirties, m/cis): Regan's suitor

Prologue

INT. THIS THEATRE'S EMPTY LOBBY OR
REHEARSAL HALL.

HENRY (actor playing Lear) and ROZ (actor playing
Goneril) are being interviewed about their upcoming pro-
duction of *King Lear*. We do not hear the interviewer's
questions. We are mid-interview.

> HENRY
>
> What is the fascination with this play?
> That's a very good question, and I think,
> really *King Lear* is about a man who
> thinks he knows the world around him. He
> has a sense of what the future holds and
> then: poof!

> ROZ
>
> It's madness, really.

> HENRY
>
> Madness, yes, that's what I'm saying, and
> we're all--well, we've talked about this a lot
> in the room--we're all intrigued by the afflic-
> tions of the mind.

> ROZ
>
> Yes, and at the beginning Goneril--

HENRY

Well, Goneril kicks it all off when Lear asks
his daughters to tell him how much they
love him. She says: "I love you more than
word can wield the matter," and then Regan:
yes, I'm "made of that same metal as my
sister," but then Cordelia--his dearest child,
whom he expects will care for him in his
old age, all she says is: "Nothing, my lord."
And Lear thinks: Nothing? What? This isn't
right. This isn't what I expected. Nothing?
Well, "Nothing will come of nothing." And
he's testing her here, he's testing the fabric
of reality, really, and reeling inside because
in that moment his whole world is turned
upside down. And in his panic to find his
footing, he opens the gates of Hell.

ROZ

And the rest of us get pulled in.

HENRY

Yes, and well, the remainder of the play is
Lear just trying to hold onto his sanity and
it's--it's profoundly moving, I think, which is
why this play is done over and over again.

ROZ

Well, yes, and it's also an incredible role for
an actor to play.

HENRY

Of course. You know, I was at the bar a few
nights ago having a beer with a couple of
friends--actors, I'm sure you know--and we

suddenly had this moment when we realized, we'd all played Lear!

ROZ

That's what I mean, like, you guys are all
legends.

HENRY

Oh, stop.

ROZ

Seriously, though, I mean you've all had the
extraordinary experience of playing Lear
and, I mean, you've all done Hamlet too,
right? There just aren't parts like that for
women.

HENRY

Oh, come on now, there's some great
Shakespearean roles for women.

ROZ

A few, yes, I know, but--

HENRY

Juliet has to be one of the greatest roles ever
written.

ROZ

Sure, but no actor playing Juliet has control
over her career. An actress is *chosen* to play
Juliet. And who knows where her career goes
from there--after she's out of ingenue range.
An actor playing Lear, on the other hand,
chooses to play that role. It's about control.

HENRY

You see why I love Roz here. Always keeps
me on my toes. You know, I don't think I'd
make it as a young actor starting out today.

ROZ

Well, I'm hardly starting out--

HENRY

Roz here has her own small theatre compa-
ny--the pieces they do--all these site-specific
things--and really good. So interesting. I'm
not as clever as all that. I wait for the phone
to ring and if it doesn't ring--that's it.

ROZ

But it does ring.

HENRY

I've been fortunate, yes, to have been offered
a number of good parts. And you grow a
little, with each one, but there's always the
fear, you know, that fear . . . I mean, with the
pandemic and all this change--good change,
so much good change--still, you can't help
but feel like your time is over, like you're no
longer needed, like there's nothing left but to
fade away . . . or . . . maybe . . .

ROZ

Which is exactly how Lear is feeling.

HENRY

What's that?

> ROZ

In the play. Lear.

> HENRY

Lear, yes Lear. It's a very rigorous part. Very athletic.

> ROZ

And Goneril--

> HENRY

Act One, you're already off to the races, and then there's the storm, of course.

> ROZ

Well, for me--

> HENRY

And just when you think you're nearing the finish line, you have to carry the girl.

> GONERIL

But Lear's attacks on Goneril are / the reason--

> HENRY

Horrendous, yes, he's vicious.

> GONERIL

Which is why / she--

> HENRY

It's no wonder you become such a bitch.

Beat.

ROZ

Wow.

HENRY

Oh . . . I didn't . . .

ROZ

Wow.

HENRY

I'm sorry if I . . . I shouldn't have . . .

ROZ

Well if I had more text I might be able to
understand why Goneril acts the way she
does, but as it is, I have to imagine--I've had
to invent some sort of backstory. I can just
. . . I can see her so clearly. Goneril.

Camera focuses on ROZ. Lights start to rise on Goneril and
fade in the house.

ROZ (CONT.)

It's seven or eight years before the play
begins and she isn't malicious. She's not
power-hungry or manipulative. I see opti-
mism. I see fierce intelligence. I see an
ambitious woman--and I mean ambitious in
a good way; in a way we find reassuring in a
leader. And she is ready to lead. Yes. Goneril
is ready to be Queen.

Act 1

Scene 1

GONERIL looks at the audience.

GONERIL: It is out of love I want my father to retire.
He has ruled this kingdom with a steady hand,
brought prosperity to those who were suffering,
and united a people divided by faction and allegiance.

Why only a few months ago, he won a war,
after which, he instructed his general to bring back the bodies
of three hundred soldiers to give them a proper burial.
How noble is that?
But like every recent gesture of kingliness,
he stopped short of completing the task.

The earth was too frozen to bury the soldiers immediately,
so they were piled in a heap just outside the palace walls.
Over the winter, the bodies congealed into an icy mound,
but now that the rains have come, they've become vulnerable
to the assaults of rats and other scavengers.

Old age, it seems, has deprived my father of his senses.
He no longer smells the decomposing corpses,
no longer feels the unrest of the peasants,
no longer sees the dissension in his ranks,
nor hears his daughters pace the upstairs corridors
waiting for spring to come.

It's not that I'm desperate for the responsibilities of a sovereign.
As I am woman, I question my own ambition.
Who am I to carry forward my father's legacy?
How dare I presume to lead a nation?

But as I am human, I question my hesitation.
If not me, then who?
If not now, then when?
How dare I stand idly by
knowing there is something that can be done.

I have been staying at the palace these past two months
to encourage my father to find peace in his sunset years,
to initiate the path of succession,
to relinquish his kingdom and leave its future to me.
Out of love, you understand.
Only love.

Scene 2

OLENA *dresses* GONERIL.

GONERIL: This corset is too tight.

OLENA: I'm sorry, my lady.

GONERIL: It's pinching my skin.

OLENA: My sincere apologies.

OLENA *loosens it.*

Is that better?

GONERIL: No.

She loosens it further.

OLENA: How about that?

GONERIL: No.

She removes GONERIL's corset.

OLENA: This?

GONERIL: Better, yes.
But my skirts.

OLENA: What's wrong with your skirts?

GONERIL: They're itching my legs.

OLENA loosens GONERIL's skirts.

OLENA: Better?

GONERIL: No.

Loosens more.

OLENA: Better?

GONERIL: No.

The skirts drop to the floor.

OLENA: Better?

GONERIL: You're a terrible lady's maid.

OLENA: Then why do you keep me around?

GONERIL: You have other talents.

> *OLENA slides her hand into GONERIL's underclothes.*
> *They start to have sex.*
> *REGAN bounds in.*

REGAN: You'll never believe what I just heard.

GONERIL: Don't you ever knock?

REGAN: Kent's on his way back so I think you should talk to him about the best way to / approach Father—

GONERIL: I'm getting dressed, Regan.

REGAN: So?

GONERIL: So I'd like a bit of privacy.

REGAN: Why? I've seen it all before. And honestly, you've got nothing to be embarrassed about.

GONERIL: Regan!

REGAN: Well, maybe that birthmark on your right buttock.

GONERIL: Get out.

REGAN: Fine! Clearly you don't want my help!

> *REGAN storms out.*

OLENA: We need to go home.

GONERIL: Not yet.

OLENA: It's been two months.

GONERIL: I'm so close.

OLENA: Albany will be back from Spain any day now and instead of taking advantage of this time alone, we've spent it here in your childhood bedroom.

GONERIL: I think we've managed to make it work.

OLENA: I'm serious.

GONERIL: So am I. My father's almost there, I can feel it. Just yesterday he said I have a better head for numbers than he does.

OLENA: Sure, but there's never been a queen on the throne.

GONERIL: Well, my mother.

OLENA: Your mother sat *beside* the throne.

GONERIL: Advising my father on every decision he made.

OLENA: But that's not what you want.

GONERIL: I want the next logical step.

OLENA: But does your father? Do the lords? Do the courtiers?

GONERIL: Technically, it was part of my dowry.

OLENA: Then why does he hesitate?

GONERIL: He's just making sure I'm ready.

OLENA: I don't like to see you disappointed.

GONERIL: Then get back to being a terrible lady's maid.

They kiss.

OLENA: Do you think of him?

GONERIL: My father?

OLENA: Your husband. When you and I are together.

GONERIL: Never.

OLENA: But still, you lie with him.

GONERIL: Out of duty.

OLENA: His body has things my body never will.

GONERIL: His body is only a proxy for yours.

OLENA: Then stop sleeping with him.

GONERIL: And lose everything?

OLENA: All I care about is you.

GONERIL: And I, you.

OLENA: If that were true, you would never have married him.

GONERIL: I thought we were done with jealousy.

OLENA: Easy for you to say.

GONERIL: Come on.

OLENA: You have it both ways.

GONERIL: Everything I do, I do for us.

OLENA: I don't care about a kingdom.

GONERIL: You have to care about this kingdom.

OLENA: Why?

GONERIL: Because this kingdom is me. The language, the people, the towns, the rivers, the earth itself is in my blood and I can't turn my back on it, not now when everything's falling apart, when there's a pile of bodies outside the palace walls.

Beat.

OLENA: You're amazing, you know that?

They kiss.

GONERIL: When I'm Queen, I promise you won't even see Albany.

OLENA: You'll poison him?

GONERIL: Send him off on diplomatic missions.

OLENA: To plague-infested countries?

GONERIL: Be nice.

OLENA: He's a milk-livered man.

GONERIL: And easy to control.

OLENA: A moral fool.

GONERIL: Who pacifies my father.

OLENA: And will make you an heir.

GONERIL: Eventually.

OLENA: Timing your encounters is not a foolproof way to prevent pregnancy.

GONERIL: If I can make people feel safe and cared for again, this kingdom will thrive. I know it will. And after that, I'll make space for motherhood. We'll have it all: a kingdom, a family, a future.

Scene 3

Transition to the throne room.
LEAR *and* GLOUCESTER *have been playing chess.*
The OLD WOMAN *serves food.*
GONERIL *joins them.*

LEAR: You let me win!

GLOUCESTER: I would never do that, Your Majesty.

LEAR: Then why did I win?

GLOUCESTER: I didn't notice your rook.

LEAR: Is that so?
(*a prompt*) Goneril?

GONERIL: Know the deceits of thy closest friends.

GLOUCESTER: Deceits?!

GONERIL: Know the strengths of thine enemy.

GLOUCESTER: I'm hardly your enemy.

LEAR: You are an exceptional strategist, Gloucester.

GLOUCESTER: Thank you, sir.

LEAR: Which is why you are my strategist.

The king eats.

GLOUCESTER: Yes, sir.

GONERIL: Which is why you never lose at chess, which is why my father never beats you, which is why he now wants to know why you let him win.

LEAR: You're trying to butter me up.

GLOUCESTER: I would never do such a thing.

GONERIL: You brought him flowers when you requested more funds from the treasury.

LEAR: Ah ha!

GONERIL: You served him cake when you broke the news about his hound.

LEAR: She's got your number, Gloucester.

GLOUCESTER: Just because I am a generous man doesn't mean—

LEAR: Why is this bread so hard?!!!!

OLD WOMAN: Forgive me, Your Majesty.

LEAR: I can't lose any more fillings to your rock-hard bread!

OLD WOMAN: Of course not, Your Majesty. It's only we've been given orders to bring out the day-old if it's not been touched.

LEAR: Whatever for?

OLD WOMAN: To make it stretch.

LEAR: Make it stretch?

OLD WOMAN: The bread, Your Highness.

LEAR: Who the devil instructed you to do that?

GLOUCESTER: You remember the harvest wasn't as strong as it has been in previous years.

LEAR: Is this why I won at chess?

GLOUCESTER: The floods in the spring, the drought in the summer, and then with the war—

LEAR: The war we won.

GLOUCESTER: Yes, Your Majesty.

LEAR: The war was necessary.

GLOUCESTER: Yes, sir, but—

LEAR: Do you think I would have sacrificed so many young men were it not absolutely necessary?

GONERIL: That's not what Gloucester is saying.

LEAR: Then what on earth is he saying?

GONERIL: Only that many of the young men were absent during the harvest so as winter draws to an end, food is running scarce.

LEAR: And?

GONERIL: And if we don't want the peasants to starve, we need to import more grain from the continent, which is why we really shouldn't prolong talks with the French ambassador any longer.

LEAR: Prolong?! Who's prolonging? I've wined and dined him all week.

GONERIL: But we've still made very little progress in the negotiation of our lapsed trade agreements.

LEAR: Bah!

GONERIL: He's impatient to iron out the details and get back to France.

LEAR: His father never balked at a free meal.

GONERIL: Yes, but you know young people today.

LEAR: All business, no pleasure.

GONERIL: Guilty as charged!

LEAR: Ha. Haha!

GONERIL: I can meet with him this afternoon, Father, and try to move things forward?

Beat.

LEAR: Didn't I tell you, Gloucester.

GLOUCESTER: What's that, Your Majesty?

LEAR: The future is in good hands.

GONERIL: Thank you, Father. On that subject, I was wondering—

LEAR: Has that case of wine arrived from your estate yet, Gloucester?

GLOUCESTER: Ah, yes, sir. Just this morning.

LEAR: Well then. Let's have a look.

GLOUCESTER: Oh, yes. Right away.

GLOUCESTER exits.
Beat.

GONERIL: Father, I just want to tell you how much I've learned these past couple of months.

LEAR: Good. Good.

GONERIL: I hope you have been impressed with my progress.

LEAR: You're a chip off the old block—too bad for you, my little lambkin.

GONERIL: Ah ha! Good. Good. I was wondering, then, if we might start talking about a transition plan.

LEAR: Oh?

GONERIL: Start slowly, of course. Gradually acclimatize the people to a new—

Hands bound, CORDELIA *is frogmarched into the throne room by* REGAN.

REGAN: I intend to prove, beyond a shadow of a doubt, that this man here stabbed his wife to death.

GONERIL: Not now, Regan.

REGAN: But murder is a grave offence.

GONERIL: Father and I are in the middle of something.

LEAR: No no no, not murder again.

REGAN: Arson?

LEAR: Too easy.

REGAN: Treason?

LEAR: Perhaps. What do you think, Goneril?

GONERIL: I think, Father, it would be nice if you and I could continue our serious conversation.

LEAR: What could be more serious than mediating the disputes of your subjects?

REGAN: Well said, Father.

GONERIL: Regan.

LEAR: This man here was caught stealing his neighbour's livestock.

REGAN: That's it! This peasant stole his neighbour's cow.

CORDELIA: It was a pig, actually.

LEAR: Good detail, Cordelia.

REGAN: Yes, because the pigs remind you of your dead wife.

CORDELIA: That's not what I meant.

GONERIL: Father, please—

LEAR: Go on, Goneril. The court is waiting.

> *Beat.*
> GONERIL *becomes a lawyer and* LEAR *becomes the judge.*

GONERIL: I here take my oath before this honourable assembly, that this man's neighbour began to notice his pigs disappearing one by one. However, as the neighbour couldn't make it to court today—

REGAN: *(becoming the neighbour)* So sorry I'm late, Your Honour. If it please you to hear my case, I looked out me window and saw this man crawling around in pig shit—oh shit—am I allowed to say shit in the presence of the king?

LEAR: I will allow it.

REGAN: Thank you, gracious King, because it was shit this man was crawling in.

CORDELIA: No, I wasn't.

REGAN: And then I saw him steal my pig!

CORDELIA: I—

REGAN: I demand he be hung at once!

CORDELIA: I—

LEAR: For thieving?

REGAN: It was my prize piggie!

GONERIL: And what was his reason? What was his need?

REGAN: Oh, reason not the need!

OLD WOMAN: (*aside to* CORDELIA) Perhaps he was starving.

CORDELIA: Yes, I was starving.

OLD WOMAN: Perhaps his children were starving.

CORDELIA: My children were starving.

REGAN: But he stole several of my pigs and sold them at market a few villages away. He's made a bloody business out of it!

LEAR: Let us hear what the man has to say.

CORDELIA: Please, sir, please. It was to feed my family. I'm a poor man and my wife died giving birth to our sixth child. I only wanted to put food in their mouths. Please. I won't thieve again.

LEAR: If every thief were this angelic, the prisons would be empty. Well played, my dearest.

CORDELIA: Thank you, Father.

LEAR: Now, how about a kiss for the old judge.

CORDELIA kisses her father.

So, Goneril, what shall we do with this man?

GONERIL: Tell him to repay his neighbour.

REGAN: That's it?!

CORDELIA: Thank you.

REGAN: But the sentence for thieving is a severed hand.

GONERIL: Then how will he work?

REGAN: At the very least let him be whipped.

GONERIL: If we impose a harsher sentence, we punish his children who will have no recourse but to thieve themselves.

LEAR: You'd break the cycle?

GONERIL: Try at least.

LEAR: A nice sentiment, lambkin, but in practice I think you'll find—

GLOUCESTER returns with the wine.

GLOUCESTER: Here we are, Your Majesty.

GONERIL: It's not yet noon, Father.

LEAR: Just a taste.

GLOUCESTER: (*presenting the wine*) First, you must breathe it in.

LEAR: Lovely.

GLOUCESTER: Now, swirl it in the glass and take a sip. Let it rest in your mouth for just a moment, enliven your taste buds, and then . . .

LEAR: Wonderful. Simply wonderful.

REGAN: Can I try?

LEAR: Next case!

REGAN: (*a new character*) Lechery! I'm a handsome fella so the maidens are always throwing themselves at me. Is it my fault I went after one who now says she didn't want it? Is it my fault she's with child? Is it my fault she's showing signs of some venereal disease?

CORDELIA: Ew!

GONERIL: This incident wouldn't come before the court.

REGAN: Ah, but her father is wealthy, you see, and that makes all the difference.

   KENT arrives.

KENT: There's the faces I've missed so much.

GONERIL: Dear Kent! You've made it back to us in one piece. We were starting to worry you'd lost your way.

KENT: I'd never lose my way back to my three beauties.

LEAR: Don't you mean four?

KENT: Your Majesty is good for many things. Pleasing the eye is not one of them.

GONERIL: He's back five minutes, Father, and already insulting you!

LEAR: One can't expect more from a scurvy knave.

KENT: Says the old stock-fish.

LEAR: You cozening rogue!

KENT: You festering plague-sore!

REGAN: I'd throw him in the stocks if I were you, Father.

KENT: Such cruelty! Thank Apollo for one gentle sister.

CORDELIA: I do hope you'll be staying a while.

KENT: I'd stay a year if invited so sweetly.

CORDELIA: Then stay a year. It does my father good to have you around.

KENT: It does us all good to be in your presence, my lady.

KENT presents CORDELIA with a small box.

CORDELIA: For me?

KENT: Open it.

She opens the lid. It plays music.

GONERIL: Is that Mother's music box?

REGAN: Let me see.

GONERIL: Listen.

> *They do.*
> *A song plays.*

REGAN: She used to sing us to sleep with this song.

CORDELIA: Really?

REGAN: Shhhh.

> *They listen.*

LEAR: Where did you get this?

KENT: Your wife gave it to me after my first victory. A little thank you, I believe, for bringing you home in one piece. I figured, well, since Cordelia seems to have inherited her mother's musical talent, it would be right for her to have it.

CORDELIA: Oh, thank you. Thank you.

> *She embraces KENT.*

KENT: Well, go on then, Cordelia. Won't you give us a song?

CORDELIA: If it pleases you, my lord.

> *CORDELIA prepares her instrument (a piano or a stringed*
> *instrument).*
> *KENT takes the glass of wine out of GLOUCESTER's hand.*

KENT: Cheers, mate.

KENT gulps it back.

Not bad.

CORDELIA sings a sweet song.
It is simple, clear, and pretty.

CORDELIA: (*singing*) My hands are soft, thy limbs are weary,
I will comfort thee.
My voice is clear, thine eyes are bleary,
I will comfort thee.
I will foresee thy every need,
Before it weighs upon thee.
Thy soul is tired, but I am cheery,
I will comfort thee.

Scene 4

REGAN speaks to the audience.

REGAN: Cordelia's such a suck.
Always smiling away like a lunatic.
And Goneril acts like she's so superior,
prancing after Father from one room to the next
in her transparent effort to relieve him of his crown—
which might, I admit, be a good thing for everyone—
but watching her try to ingratiate herself to him
by parroting his thoughts or mimicking the inflection of his voice
or sitting or striding or laughing the same way that he does
is driving me insane!

She wasn't always like this.
We weren't always like this.
After our mother died,

Goneril and I were inseparable.
We ate together, slept together,
snuck out into the woods and built our own little playhouse,
far away from the emptiness
our mother's death had left behind.
We knew each other completely
and that felt
so
good.

I understand, of course,
that Goneril's changed over time, but so have I.
I'm smarter.
I'm fuller.
More self-sufficient, and Father and I have all sorts of conversations
about the world and our place in it and we laugh
about the courtiers—those gilded butterflies
who flap about trying to win his favour—
I could help Goneril, really, if she'd listen, but she won't,
so I revert to playing the clown,
the only role that's ever been fully mine.
It makes me want to scream.
Or break things.
Or release these yearnings that are bubbling up from underneath;
this tingling that changes the way that I breathe,
the way I move in the world.

I long to touch and be touched.
I want to sweat and be hunted.
I need to writhe with heat,
and that desire is seeping through my pores.
I want a man to smell it.
To need it.
To surrender himself to me.

Scene 5

*EDMUND and REGAN make out in the wine cellar.
She starts to undo his pants.*

EDMUND: Wait . . . wait a minute.
Hold on.

REGAN: What's wrong?

EDMUND: Nothing, but—

REGAN: Let's do it.

EDMUND: We shouldn't.

REGAN: You don't want to?

EDMUND: I do, yes, of course I do.

REGAN: Then let's go.

EDMUND: No, Regan.

REGAN: Come on.

EDMUND: I said no.

REGAN: What's the matter?

EDMUND: It's not right.

REGAN: Yes, it is.

EDMUND: None of this is right.

REGAN: Edmund—

EDMUND: We should be in a bed, at least.

REGAN: A gentleman, now, are you?

EDMUND: Or by a warm fire.

REGAN: Or in a wine cellar.

EDMUND: I—

REGAN: It's nice and damp down here.

EDMUND: I'm sorry.

REGAN: I'm ready. I want this.

EDMUND: Me too, believe me.

REGAN: Then what's the problem?

EDMUND: I will not make another bastard.

    Beat.

REGAN: That's what you're thinking about right now?

EDMUND: I'm serious.

REGAN: You won't.

EDMUND: I might.

REGAN: Then we'll get married.
Problem solved.

EDMUND: Right. I'm sure your father would be thrilled for you to marry a bastard.

REGAN: My father has forgotten I exist. And while I pace the corridors waiting for him to find me a husband, a husband who won't be nearly as handsome as you, I am going mad. I'm shrivelling in this palace waiting for something to do with this body. I want you, Edmund.

EDMUND: I want you too.

REGAN: Every part of me wants every part of you.

EDMUND: Yes.

REGAN: Now.

She tries again.
He's tempted but pulls back.

EDMUND: You know, my father introduces me to everyone we meet.

REGAN: That's a good thing.

EDMUND: Even when I've met that person about a hundred times before, he says: "Have you met my son, Edmund?"

REGAN: So, he's proud of you.

EDMUND: He's proud of himself. He does it so he can make some joke about how much fun it was to conceive me: even though I'm a base, half-blooded bastard, there was good sport at my making.

What's more, he wants everyone to know that he's a man who takes responsibility for his sins. He owns his mistakes.

REGAN: Well, I'll take Gloucester's mistake over his lawful progeny any day.

EDMUND: Don't talk about Edgar.

REGAN: He's such a dweeb.

EDMUND: A legitimate dweeb.

REGAN: Who's enjoying himself in France.

EDMUND: Actually, he's coming home tomorrow.

REGAN: He's had his fill of French wine and women?

EDMUND: More likely he's exhausted the library.

REGAN: And least your sibling doesn't scold you like a child.

EDMUND: Goneril's just looking out for you.

REGAN: She's protecting her own image. Like anything that comes out of my mouth is going to reflect badly on her so she's constantly trying to push me into the shadows.

EDMUND: You could never live in the shadows.

REGAN: And yet, that's where our future queen would prefer that I stay.

EDMUND: You're the one who should be Queen.

REGAN: Treason!

EDMUND: People don't need a monarch who can recite the civil code or rattle off the finances. They want someone with energy. Someone with imagination. Someone with pizzazz.

REGAN: Pizzazz?!

EDMUND: Yeah, pizzazz.

REGAN: Well, if it's pizzazz you're after.

She draws him close.

EDMUND: Hey now, what did we just say?

REGAN: Nothing about wandering hands.

They go at it again.

Act 2

Scene 1

OLENA dresses GONERIL for hunting—she hurries.
REGAN lurks in the doorway.

GONERIL: I thought he'd never stop talking.

OLENA: Don't rush or you'll tear something.

GONERIL: French is such an unnecessarily long language. It's all of that "politesse": Je voudrais commencer par vous remercier de m'avoir invité— Not that jacket, Olena.

OLENA: Why don't you just wear what you usually wear?

GONERIL: Because I usually hunt on my own.

OLENA: And?

GONERIL: Men are easily startled.

OLENA: By a woman wearing pants?

REGAN: You're wasting your time—they've already left.

GONERIL: I'll catch up.

REGAN: If you can find them.

GONERIL: I know where Father likes to go.

REGAN: You're trying too hard.

GONERIL: Hurry up, Olena.

REGAN: It irritates him.

GONERIL: And you are irritating me.

REGAN: Good comeback.

> *Beat.*

No one likes a kiss-ass.

GONERIL: I'm not a kiss-ass.

REGAN: Ha!

> *Beat.*

GONERIL: You don't need to be in here.

REGAN: But I'm helping.

GONERIL: (*to* OLENA) Other hat.

OLENA: How am I supposed to know what a hunting outfit looks like!

REGAN: (*passing* OLENA *the right hat*) This one, Olena. Obviously.

GONERIL: I'm just trying to prove to Father that I'm ready to lead.

REGAN: By being a kiss-ass.

GONERIL: If being attentive makes me a kiss-ass, if studying Father's diplomatic and military accomplishments makes me a kiss-ass, if contemplating a prosperous future for our kingdom makes me a kiss-ass, then yes, Regan, yes, I'm a kiss-ass.

Beat.

REGAN: Father hates a kiss-ass.

GONERIL: Well maybe if you hadn't interrupted this morning when I was right on the cusp of having a serious—

REGAN: You weren't on the cusp of anything, Goneril.

GONERIL: Then what do you think I should do, huh? What's your brilliant idea?

REGAN: Just cut the bullshit and get to the truth.

GONERIL: The truth? I'll tell you the truth. I meet with powerful men every day to try to resolve any number of problems. And if a man like the French ambassador compliments my dress, my smile, and my "exotic heritage" as he did today, how should I truthfully respond? The truth is that I want to tell him to wipe that smirk off his face, that my dress and my smile don't belong to him, that my "exotic heritage" has nothing to do with importing grain and livestock so can he please stop leering at me so we can get back to discussing our lapsed trade agreement.

REGAN: Okay, I get it.

GONERIL: However, another truth in that moment is that he needs me to make him feel confident, to make him feel desired. The truth then follows, that if I do not affirm his virility, the chances of us having a productive conversation will be greatly reduced so I must respond to his seeming compliment with a laugh or a quip.

REGAN: I get it.

GONERIL: Which leads me to my final truth: I need to play the game. I need to give him what he wants, all the while projecting clear boundaries so he doesn't get the wrong idea, in order to get on with our conversation, and each calculated response, each curated movement is a necessary step in the right direction.

CORDELIA enters.

CORDELIA: Can I come hunting too?

GONERIL: Not today, Cordelia.

CORDELIA: I won't get in the way.

REGAN: You're already in the way.

CORDELIA: But I can help you convince Father to retire.

REGAN: You were eavesdropping again.

CORDELIA: I wasn't.

REGAN: Always lurking around corners.

GONERIL: Pass me my gloves, Cordelia.

CORDELIA: You can tell me things. I'm not a child anymore.

REGAN: Finally started to bleed, have you?

GONERIL: (*slightly amused*) Regan.

CORDELIA: I can help you if you let me.

REGAN: By playing one of your pretty songs?

CORDELIA: By showing Father how much we love him.

> *REGAN makes a barfing sound.*
> *GONERIL laughs.*

I just . . . I only meant . . . His sadness is so deep that he seems lost sometimes. It's like he's balancing on a ledge just outside the window and if you startle him, he'll fall so you have to reach out slowly to lead him back inside.

> *Beat.*

REGAN: Cordelia the poet!

CORDELIA: Oh . . . no . . . I mean . . . I'm sorry, I just—

GONERIL: Don't apologize.

CORDELIA: I'm sorry, I mean—

GONERIL: You make yourself small when you apologize.

CORDELIA: Yes, I know, I was just thinking if we could find a way to make Father happy then—

GONERIL: You already do that, little one. Father only has to look at you and a smile spreads across his face.

CORDELIA: And you both despise me for that.

GONERIL: Of course we don't.

REGAN: It just gives us a bit of a toothache.

CORDELIA: What do you mean?

REGAN: (*to* GONERIL) Right at the back, you know?

GONERIL *smirks.*

CORDELIA: (*to* REGAN) What do you mean?

REGAN: You're just so dang sweet.

The OLD WOMAN *enters.*

OLD WOMAN: I've packed you a few supplies, my lady. The water might still be a little warm and taste of smoke, but I thought it wise to boil it, what with peasants falling ill.

GONERIL: What are you talking about?

OLD WOMAN: Mostly just starvation, my lady, which isn't cause for alarm, of course, but there's been some talk of disease on account of the rotting—

GONERIL: The rotting?

OLD WOMAN: Bodies, my lady, which is why priests are insisting on daily ceremonies.

GONERIL: Congregating spreads infection.

OLD WOMAN: Only way to keep people calm, I'm afraid. Priests get loud when kings are silent.

GONERIL: Your king is never silent.

OLD WOMAN: Of course not, my lady.

GONERIL: (*finding bread in the satchel*) Why do you keep plying me with burnt bread?

OLD WOMAN: Pardon me, Your Majesty-In-Waiting, it's only, well, I remember the crispy bits used to settle my tum when I was with child. The nausea will go away after the first few months, which, I'm sure you'll find difficult to believe right now, but it really does ease up.

Beat.

REGAN: Are you pregnant?!

GONERIL: No!

OLD WOMAN: Dearest apologies, I had no idea your lady's maid was such a treasure.

GONERIL: What?

OLD WOMAN: I've just never met a lady's maid who'd clean her mistress's bloody rags. You've been here two moons, you see, and not a soiled undergarment has come my way, so naturally, I assumed—

GONERIL: Get out.

OLD WOMAN: You mustn't blame an old woman for her attentive nature.

REGAN: Goneril—

GONERIL: Get out. All of you. And not a word to anyone!

The OLD WOMAN, REGAN, and CORDELIA leave.

Shit.

OLENA: Wow.

GONERIL: I'm running out of time. I thought this would all be easier.

OLENA: Were you planning on telling me?

GONERIL: I just . . . I couldn't talk about it.

OLENA: We said: no secrets.

GONERIL: I was going to tell you.

OLENA: But you didn't.

GONERIL: I needed time.

OLENA: I'm such a fool.

GONERIL: No no no, listen, please. I was scared, all right. I was terrified when I thought I might be . . . I knew if I talked about it, if I said it out loud, it would all be real and I'd feel so weak.

OLENA: Weak?

GONERIL: Like those women confined to bedchambers with midwives buzzing around. Please, Olena, I need your help. If my father learns I'm . . . then, he'll only see me as a queen mother rather than a queen and that would be the end.

OLENA: Of what?

GONERIL: Of me.

Beat.

OLENA: Regan's right, you know.

GONERIL: About what?

OLENA: If you're going to convince King Lear to relinquish his crown, you've got to stop being so deferential.

GONERIL: No more secrets, I promise.

OLENA: You need to charge into the fray.

GONERIL: Yes, yes, I will.

OLENA: No fear. No hesitation.

GONERIL: Ready to kill.

Scene 2

The OLD WOMAN sifts through a chamber pot of shit with her bare hands.

OLD WOMAN: You find me a woman who's raised four sons and sent 'em off to be slaughtered at war, raised three daughters only to have 'em all die in childbirth, been told where to go and what to do by men that range from husband to king, and I'll show you a woman who will dig through a bowl of shit to find a bit of gold she knows is there.

Valuable things get swallowed every day.

I've heard many a man justify ignoble deeds with noble words. I've seen a man cheat another out of his livelihood then turn around and blame him for pinching a loaf of bread. I've seen a man accuse a woman of lustiness even whilst he's giving her a poke. I've seen a king sit on his throne pretending not to know when his usefulness is spent, so why shouldn't I serve a bit of hard bread, a bit of tough meat, a bit of sticky toffee to loosen a treasure that's longing to break free.

And when it does, oh but he complains. Course, I stand by making sounds of sympathy women learn early in life:

> Awwww, you poor dear.
> Ohhhhh, that must hurt.
> Oooooo, let me fix you a cold compress.

(*finding a filling*) Ah ha! Takes a lack of dignity to find a gold filling in kingly excrement. That's women's work though, isn't it? To take a bowl of shit and find something that glimmers, something that makes the pain of having to put up with it all just about worthwhile.

Scene 3

LEAR, KENT, and GLOUCESTER hunt in the woods.
EDMUND trails behind with the equipment.

LEAR: So what did he look like?

KENT: Who?

LEAR: Their general. The one you beheaded.

KENT: Oh, now he was a brazen-faced varlet.

LEAR: Go on.

KENT: A base rascal.

LEAR: And?

KENT: A clamorous ruffian.
A rump-fed swollen parcel of dropsies.

LEAR: He was wart-nosed, wasn't he?

KENT: Indeed he was, Your Majesty. A wart-nosed, long-tongued bolting hutch of beastliness; a wild-eyed, knit-browed knave; a sour-breathed whoreson of a mongrel bitch couched on a festering dung-heap; the rankest compound of villainous stench. And when I hacked that monster's head from his neck, his infected blood sprayed into my mouth so I could taste his sour defeat.

GLOUCESTER: Thank you for that image.

LEAR: Ah, I do miss it. The adrenaline. The clash of swords. Smell of the battle.

KENT: Better than the smell of rotting corpses.

LEAR: Ha ha! . . . What's that?

KENT: You are pleased with the way our campaign ended?

LEAR: You doubt my praise?

KENT: Never, sir. It's only that the men who got back before me say they haven't yet received their gold.

LEAR: You reassured them, of course.

KENT: You're good for it, sir, I know, but with the way things are.

LEAR: And just how are things?

KENT: Well, coming back to their families who suffered through the long winter.

LEAR: I hear what you're saying.

KENT: Good, sir.

LEAR: Coming home is always a disappointment after the excitement of war.

KENT: Ah—

LEAR: A morale boost. That's what they need. Bring your men up to the palace this evening and we'll give them a proper celebration.

KENT: That's very kind of you, sir. Then perhaps tomorrow we can talk about the casualties.

LEAR: Casualties?

KENT: We need to bury the fallen soldiers.

LEAR: Of course, I know, of course. I'm the one who ordered them home.

KENT: Yes, sir, but—

LEAR: Tomorrow, tomorrow. We'll talk about it tomorrow.

GONERIL arrives.

GONERIL: I'd always wondered about the mysteries of men and their hunting expeditions. Now I see it's all a ruse so you can stand around gossiping like a group of schoolgirls!

LEAR: Oh no! She's caught us!

KENT: Thank the gods you're here, my lady. This conversation needs some elevating. Recite us a speech or something.

GONERIL: A speech?

KENT: Or a bit of poetry, maybe.

GONERIL: Poetry. Poetry, yes, I think I know one that will suit you lads.

A woman I knew was quite blunt.
She wanted to go out and hunt.
The men were polite,
They didn't dare fight,
But they treated her just like a cun—try woman.

KENT: Ohhhhh!!!

The men laugh.

LEAR: My daughters don't take kindly to being left out.

KENT: Have you shot that rifle before?

GONERIL: Many times.

KENT: The thing to know about a rifle is that it gives quite a kickback.

GONERIL: I know.

KENT: It's important to brace yourself before you shoot.

GONERIL: Thank you.

KENT: Here, let me load it for you.

He takes her rifle.

GONERIL: I know how to—

KENT: You gotta go to half-cock, open the breech, load the round /
into the chamber—

EDMUND: Goneril shot a stag last week.

KENT: Did she now?

EDMUND: It was a difficult shot to make.

KENT: You do know it's cheating if the stag's already mounted on
the wall.

GONERIL: Unless you're the one who shot it. In which case, it might
not yet be dead.

They laugh.

LEAR: What do you say we shoot something now?

KENT: By all means, Your Majesty.

LEAR: It's a perfect day for it.

GLOUCESTER: A bit cold if you ask me.

KENT: That's only because you prefer to be squeezed between a fat pair of thighs at all times.

(*clocking* GONERIL) Pardon me, my lady.

GONERIL: I'll not fault a man for pleasure, so long as he tarries where the pleasant fountains flow.

KENT: There's nothing Gloucester loves more than a pleasant fountain!

GLOUCESTER: I'll only say: some of us have to pick up the slack when the men go off to war.

KENT: And I'll only say: poor ladies.

LEAR *and* GONERIL *laugh.*

GLOUCESTER: Laugh all you like, but I've had no complaints.

KENT: I'm just a bit surprised to hear your soldier's not tired of standing at attention, old man.

GONERIL *laughs.*

GLOUCESTER: There's nothing wrong with my soldier.

KENT: Go on, give us the details.

GLOUCESTER: At least I'm a generous lover, which is more than I can say for you.

KENT: Let you down last time, did I?

GLOUCESTER: I attend to female pleasure; just ask this boy's mother.

EDMUND: Father, please.

GLOUCESTER: You have met my son, Edmund, haven't you?

KENT: Once or twice.

GLOUCESTER: I used to blush to acknowledge him, but he's turned into such an accomplished young man, despite the way he came rather saucily into the world, that I've taken him on completely.

KENT: You're a lucky bastard. Who knows how many siblings you've got crawling around in the muck.

> *They laugh.*

Gotta be at least two dozen, don't you think, sir?

> *They all look at* LEAR.
> *He's been staring off into space.*
> *He doesn't respond.*

GONERIL: Father?

LEAR: Huh?

Oh, yes yes yes.

> GONERIL *approaches her father.*

GONERIL: It's so nice to see you smiling, Father.

LEAR: I smile all the time.

GONERIL: But not like this.

LEAR: I'm out of the palace, so maybe that's it, lambkin.

GONERIL: I'm sure it is. But imagine, Father, if this was your life.

LEAR: What's that?

GONERIL: Hunting every day. With your friends.

LEAR: If only I had the time.

GONERIL: Perhaps you should make the time. I feel like you'd enjoy a life of leisure. I feel like you deserve it.

LEAR: Is that how you *feel*?

GONERIL: Why, yes.

LEAR: There's very little room for feeling in leadership, Goneril. The appearance of feeling as a tactical manoeuvre, yes, but actual feeling hinders rational decision-making.

GONERIL: It was only a figure of speech.

LEAR: It is figures of speech upon which we are judged.

GONERIL: I know, Father.

LEAR: No room for error.

GONERIL: I know.

EDMUND: *(spying a doe)* Look, look, over there, a doe.

KENT: Would you look at that beauty.

GLOUCESTER: Telescope, Edmund.

KENT: Such an elegant creature.

LEAR takes aim.

LEAR: It's not in good times you will be tested, Goneril. When you choose to sacrifice something you love for the sake of the greater good—that's when you will know the true burden of power.

> *He shoots.*
> *He's missed.*

(*outraged*) DAMN IT ALL TO HELL!!!!! How many times have I told you not to touch me when I'm shooting, Gloucester!

GLOUCESTER: But, sir, I didn't—

LEAR: Are you calling me a liar?!

GLOUCESTER: No, sir—

LEAR: That I cast blame without cause?!

GLOUCESTER: No, sir, but I—

GONERIL: (*defusing his anger*) It was the wind, Father.

LEAR: There is no wind!

GONERIL: I felt a gust just as you shot.

LEAR: You did?

GONERIL: (*a prompt*) Didn't you, Kent?

KENT: Oh. Yes. Yes.

GONERIL: There's a thickness to the air. A pressure.

LEAR: The light has changed.

GONERIL: You're right, Father. The light has changed.

LEAR: Will it rain, do you think?

GONERIL: A storm is surely brewing.

KENT: Hard to see anything in this light.

LEAR: Then let's get back to the palace. I'd hate to get caught in a storm.

> *GONERIL starts back with the men, then stalls watching them go.*
> *She looks up to the sky and sees a bird.*
> *She raises her rifle.*

Scene 4

> *CORDELIA speaks to the audience.*

CORDELIA: My sisters think I'm stupid.
They think I don't understand complicated things
because I wear a pleasant disguise.
The truth is, I'm only happy
because all the unhappy spaces in this palace
are already taken.
All the angry spaces too.
And the jealous spaces.
And the lonely spaces.
Even as a baby, I could sense the longing.

I killed my mother the day I was born
so they left me alone as a child.

Every now and then I was rocked by a nurse,
or prodded by my sisters, and if I cried,
they left me to my misery.
But if I smiled . . .

I can melt sorrow with my smile,
unfix scowls with my smile,
stop arguments with my smile.
When Father's in one of his furies,
I lay my head on his shoulder,
stroke his beard,
and draw tears of joy from his eyes.
And so, I smile.
But my sisters mock me for it.
They don't know the chore of being good,
of saying things I know that other people want to hear,
of never making trouble,
of holding in the rage.

I'm finding it harder and harder to keep the shape
that everyone expects.
There's a heaviness inside me.
Like the world is pressing in.
Like I can't be good anymore.

> GONERIL *shoots a bird from the sky.*
> CORDELIA *runs crying into her father's arms.*

Scene 5

CORDELIA: It's gone! It's gone!

LEAR, GLOUCESTER, and GONERIL enter.

LEAR: Are you sure you've looked everywhere, my love?

CORDELIA: It's gone. It's disappeared.

GONERIL: What's all the fuss about?

LEAR: Your sister's music box is missing.

GONERIL: You mean our mother's music box?!

CORDELIA: It was right on top of my dresser.

GONERIL: Where did you take it?

CORDELIA: Nowhere.

GONERIL: Where did you leave it?

CORDELIA: Nowhere.

LEAR: Calm down, Goneril.

GONERIL: I don't know why you let her have it, Father.

LEAR: It's bound to turn up.

GLOUCESTER: I've instructed the servants to check the library.

CORDELIA: I looked there already.

GONERIL: Tell them to look in the kennel too.

GLOUCESTER: Right away, my lady.

GLOUCESTER exits.

GONERIL: She was probably showing it to those stupid dogs.

CORDELIA: I wasn't.

LEAR: Have some compassion, Goneril.

GONERIL: That music box should have been entrusted to me instead of this silly little girl.

REGAN and the OLD WOMAN enter.

OLD WOMAN: It's been found, Your Majesty.

LEAR: There we are. Problem solved.

GONERIL: That music box stays with me from now on. Well? Where did she leave it?

OLD WOMAN: In my search of the palace I thought to look in the servants' quarters, as you can never be too trusting of the help, I'm afraid, and I happened to poke my head into a maid's chamber and caught a glimpse of the music box peeking out from under a pillow.

GONERIL: You're saying it was stolen?

OLD WOMAN: It looks that way, my lady.

GONERIL: Thievery is a serious offence.

OLD WOMAN: And a shocking one, at that.

GONERIL: Well, whomever it was must be punished.

OLD WOMAN: I'm glad you see it that way, my lady, because the box was found in the chamber of your lady's maid.

GONERIL: What? Olena wouldn't have stolen the music box.

LEAR: Unless, perhaps, she shared the opinion of her mistress.

GONERIL: And what opinion is that?

LEAR: That the music box should have been entrusted to you.

KENT enters with OLENA, whose hands are bound.

GONERIL: Oh, come on. Is that really necessary?

KENT: Standard procedure for thieving, isn't it? In case we have to take a finger or a hand.

GONERIL: This is ridiculous.

LEAR: Ridiculous for you and yours? Or ridiculous for all your subjects?

GONERIL: I . . . Olena, you have been accused of stealing this music box. Did you do it?

OLENA: No, my lady.

GONERIL: Then how did it make its way into your bedchamber?

OLENA: I have no idea.

GONERIL: There we are. She knows nothing about it.

LEAR: And you take her at her word?

GONERIL: I have no reason to doubt someone I have trusted for years.

LEAR: Except the evidence.

GONERIL: Brought forward by this old servant. She could have stolen it herself and claimed to have discovered it in Olena's room. Why should I trust this senile old woman over my own lady's maid?

OLD WOMAN: I couldn't agree more with your reasoning, my lady, which is why I ran straight to Lady Regan.

REGAN: I saw it there myself.

GONERIL: Well, now, isn't that convenient.

REGAN: What's that supposed to mean?

GONERIL: You've always had it out for Olena.

REGAN: You think I'd set her up?

GONERIL: I wouldn't put it past you.

REGAN: And I wouldn't put it past you to trust the word of a lady's maid over that of your own flesh and blood.

GONERIL: Olena isn't just a lady's maid.

REGAN: No? What is she then?

GONERIL: This is absurd.

LEAR: You just reminded us all that thievery is a serious offence.

GONERIL: I feel like this has to be some sort of set-up.

LEAR: Really, Goneril? Is that how you *feel?*

Beat.

GONERIL: I here take my oath before this honourable assembly that this lady's maid has been accused of thievery. Olena, please explain how the music box came to be found in your bedchamber.

OLENA: I'm not the one you should be asking.

GONERIL: Whom should I be asking?

OLENA: Those that do accuse me.

GONERIL: So you maintain your innocence.

OLENA: I do.

GONERIL: The incriminating circumstances of this situation compel me to take this accusation seriously. And yet, this woman has never before been suspected of wrongdoing, so I am hard pressed to pass a severe judgment. Therefore, a humble apology will put this all to rest.

Beat.

You may kneel and apologize.

OLENA: I will not.

GONERIL: With an apology, this episode will be behind us.

OLENA: To apologize would be to admit wrongdoing.

GONERIL: Or simply to accept that circumstances are beyond your control.

OLENA: I will not apologize for something I didn't do.

GONERIL: At the very least you are guilty of leaving your chamber door unlocked.

OLENA: Do you lock your door when you leave for the day?

GONERIL: I'm not the one on trial here.

OLENA: No, you're leading the prosecution.

GONERIL: Don't talk back to me!

Beat.

Kneel or be dismissed.

Beat.

Apologize or leave.

Beat.

OLENA: I will not, my lady.

GONERIL: Then you will pack your bags.

Act 3

Scene 1

The OLD WOMAN sings.

OLD WOMAN: Sheep in the meadow
And ducks on the pond
    With a heigh-ho, the wind and the rain
Cows out to pasture
And horses beyond
    With a heigh-ho, the wind and the rain
Dogs in their kennels
And pigs in the barn
    With a heigh-ho, the wind and the rain
My little baby's
Asleep in my arms
    With a heigh-ho, the wind and the rain
My little baby
Lies dead in my arms
    With a heigh-ho . . .

Sounds of men below, drinking.
A bedroom upstairs in the palace.
CORDELIA is in bed, maybe trying to sleep.
GONERIL reads.
REGAN does some sort of repetitive action (e.g., rocking back on a chair, tapping her fingers, clicking her tongue—whatever it is, it annoys GONERIL).

GONERIL: Could you not?

REGAN: What?

GONERIL: Make that sound.

> *REGAN stops.*
> *GONERIL resumes reading.*
> *REGAN begins another repetitive action that is even more*
> *annoying than the first.*
> *This visibly irritates GONERIL.*

Regan.

REGAN: What?

GONERIL: Honestly, how old are you?

REGAN: Old enough to know I don't have to listen to you.

> *REGAN stops doing whatever it was.*
> *Beat.*
> *She does something even more annoying.*

GONERIL: I swear to the gods, Regan, if you don't stop, I'll—

REGAN: What? Tell Father?

> *GONERIL snaps—she moves to attack REGAN.*
> *Maybe she stops herself before she gets there.*
> *Maybe she doesn't stop herself and the two wrestle like children.*

> *A crash from below.*
> *A bellow of laughter.*
> *Beat.*

CORDELIA: They're loud tonight.

GONERIL: Celebrating Kent's return.

REGAN: And we're stuck up here with the stench of death wafting through cracks in the walls.

GONERIL: Don't be disrespectful.

REGAN: Do you think if I threw myself out that window the pile of rotting men would break my fall?

CORDELIA: Ew.

GONERIL: Those men sacrificed / their lives—

REGAN: Would it be a hard landing, do you think?

GONERIL: Do you have no shame?

REGAN: Or have they melted enough to be soft. Like jumping into a bowl of pudding.

CORDELIA: We could go to my room instead.

GONERIL: My room is farthest away from the Great Hall.

REGAN: Shhhh, Goneril, they might hear you.

GONERIL: Men are unpredictable when they're drunk.

REGAN: Really? They seem to me to be completely predictable in their indifference to us hiding away up here.

GONERIL: And what does it cost you, Regan, to stay with your sisters for one evening? You don't see Cordelia complaining.

REGAN: Cordelia wouldn't complain if you cut off her arm.

CORDELIA: I'm right here.

Beat.

REGAN: It's never going to happen, you realize.

GONERIL: What?

REGAN: You: Queen.

GONERIL: If you're talking about the acceptance of a woman on the / throne—

REGAN: Don't forget about your exotic heritage.

GONERIL: This land is full of people that come from afar.

REGAN: And how many of them are in charge?

GONERIL: The only thing that should matter / is whether—

REGAN: People don't care about "should."

GONERIL: I can only focus on what I can change.

REGAN: What, like your hair?!

GONERIL: Why do you have to fight against everything?

REGAN: If things were fair, I wouldn't have to fight.

GONERIL: You're just angry because you can't go to a party.

REGAN: And why shouldn't I be.

GONERIL: Because it's selfish.

REGAN: Look who's talking.

GONERIL: Everything I do, I do for other people.

REGAN: Everything you do, you do for yourself.

GONERIL: You have no idea what it's like to try to take responsibility for this family.

REGAN: No one asked you to do that.

GONERIL: And yet it has to be done.

REGAN: You know what else has to be done?

  REGAN starts dressing.

GONERIL: What are you doing?

REGAN: Exactly what I want to do.

GONERIL: It's not safe down there.

REGAN: Oh, come off it, Goneril.

GONERIL: Men are unpredictable / when they're drunk.

REGAN: When they're drunk, yes, I know, but when do I get to be unpredictable? When do I get to follow my pleasures or passions? Why do I have to rot away up here with you two?

GONERIL: When I am Queen—

REGAN: Yes, when you are Queen, life will be sunshine and roses, but as I can't see that happening any time soon, I'm going to live while I still can.

GONERIL: You make it so difficult for people to care about you.

REGAN: At least I don't banish the people I love.

Beat.

GONERIL: Go on then, Regan!

REGAN storms out.

I'm done! I'm done with you!
Ugh!!! She makes my blood boil!

CORDELIA: She didn't mean to hurt you.

GONERIL: Of course she did. She pushes and pushes and pushes until I snap. And I fall for it every time.

CORDELIA: She's not usually like this.

GONERIL: You're saying I bring out the best in her?

CORDELIA: It's more like she's drowning right now, in a lake all alone. She's flailing her arms and crying out for you to save her. Regan is desperate for your love. She just doesn't know how to ask for it.

GONERIL: Who made you so wise?

CORDELIA smiles.

Promise me you'll never change, little one.

CORDELIA: Never sounds like a long time.

GONERIL: You are good. You are kind. The world conspires to make people bitter so you need to guard your honest heart.

CORDELIA: My honest heart?

GONERIL: That's your unique gift, Cordelia. You've got to protect it.

CORDELIA: I'll try.

GONERIL: Promise.

CORDELIA: I promise.

Scene 2

The party.
Loud music.
Talking, laughing, cheers, male voices.
REGAN approaches KENT.

REGAN: (*bowing to* KENT) May I have this dance, milady.

He laughs. They dance.

LEAR: (*to* KENT) Didn't I tell you my girls don't take kindly to being left out!

KENT: Makes a welcome change to these louts.

REGAN: All right, Father, your turn.

LEAR: I think my dancing days are through.

REGAN: We'll see about that!

> *REGAN dances with LEAR.*
> *Shift.*
> *Now REGAN and EDMUND are drinking wine off to the side.*

I should have broken out long ago.

EDMUND: It's not always this festive.

REGAN: I'll take that as a compliment.

> *REGAN drinks a glass of wine.*

EDMUND: Hey, now, slow down.

REGAN: Relax, Goneril.

EDMUND: Haha! Just promise me you'll go back upstairs if things get rough.

REGAN: *(getting close)* Why? You planning to fight over me?

EDMUND: Easy, your father will see.

REGAN: *(touching him sexually)* Did he see that, do you think?

EDMUND: Not here.

REGAN: Or that?

EDMUND: Not now. You're cut off, do you hear me?

REGAN: Dance with me at least.

EDMUND: Now that I can do.

They're about to dance when LEAR *interrupts with* CORNWALL.

LEAR: And this is my second daughter, Regan.

REGAN: (*curtsying*) The second daughter welcomes you.

CORNWALL: Then I am content.

REGAN: But who are you, my lord? You're too well dressed to have served under this ruffian.

KENT: Grrrrr!

LEAR: The Duke of Cornwall was passing through.

REGAN: The more the merrier, Duke of Cornwall.

CORNWALL: Looks like you're the merriest of them all.

REGAN: Life's too short to be sullen.

CORNWALL: And too long not to dance with the belle of the ball.

REGAN: Then you'll have to wait your turn.

> REGAN *dances with* EDMUND.
> *Shift.*
> *Now* REGAN *is in a circle of men doing impressions.*

(*imitating* CORDELIA *singing*) It's such a lovely day! I am cheerful, come what may!

LEAR: Cordelia!

REGAN: (*imitating* KENT) Has anyone seen a severed hand lying around? I've lost my good-luck charm!

GLOUCESTER: Kent!

REGAN: (*imitating* GONERIL) Reign yourself in, Regan. If you don't take yourself seriously, no one else will!

KENT: Goneril!

GLOUCESTER: And what about me, then. Let's see your best Earl of Gloucester.

REGAN: I'm afraid not, my lord.

GLOUCESTER: Not impressionable enough, am I?

REGAN: I only imitate fools.

> *Dancing starts up again.*
> *Shift.*
> KENT *is doing push-ups.*

MEN: Ninety-eight, ninety-nine, one hundred!

> KENT *stands, victorious.*
> *A cheer.*

REGAN: Shame on you all. Cheering for something that requires so little effort.

KENT: Oh, really?

REGAN: You're only lifting your own weight, after all.

KENT: And whose weight should I be lifting?

> *She smiles.*
> *The men cheer.*

Right, then, go on. I'll earn my next round.

> KENT *gets back into push-up position.*
> REGAN *perches on his back.*
> *The men cheer.*

MEN: One. Two. Three!

Scene 3

> REGAN *enters the cellar.*
> *She's drunk and giddy.*
> *She sings a raunchy pub song as she strips.*

REGAN: (*singing*) "When she looks you in the eye,
You will know the reason why
You cannot turn away.
She has cast her wicked spell
And your heart will start to swell
You will never get away."

Come out, come out wherever you are.
I know you're somewhere . . .
I know you're watching me . . .
There's nowhere to hide down here.

> GLOUCESTER *steps into the light.*

GLOUCESTER: I suppose you're right.

> REGAN *scrambles to put her clothes back on.*

REGAN: Oh . . . oh! Oh, my gods . . .

GLOUCESTER: I didn't mean to startle you.

REGAN: I'm . . . I'm so sorry, my lord.

GLOUCESTER: It's quite all right.

REGAN: I only . . . I thought you were someone else.

GLOUCESTER: Too bad for me.

REGAN: Oh . . . uh . . .

GLOUCESTER: Kidding, of course.

REGAN: Yes . . . well . . . yes, I—

She bursts out laughing.

This is—I'm really sorry, my lord. I'm going to go now.

She stumbles.

GLOUCESTER: *(helping her)* Easy . . .

REGAN: What are you doing down here anyway?

GLOUCESTER: I needed a moment.

REGAN: To hide in a corner and jump out at an unsuspecting maiden?

GLOUCESTER: Well, haha, no, no, I just wanted a bit of quality time with the good stuff.

REGAN: Oh, your fancy wine.

GLOUCESTER: If I drink it upstairs, Kent will gulp it all back.

REGAN: He really is like a fish. Like a big . . . harmless . . . fish.

GLOUCESTER: The worst of it is, he has an undiscerning tongue.

REGAN: What do you mean?

GLOUCESTER: What sort of a tongue have you?

REGAN: Huh?

GLOUCESTER: For wine, my dear.

REGAN: Oh, I never drink wine, my lord. I'm a good little princess.

GLOUCESTER: Are you now? Well, I firmly believe every queen should be able to distinguish a sophisticated northern Italian grape from the plonk that passes for table wine around here. Try this.

REGAN: Well . . . if you insist . . . just this once.

GLOUCESTER: It'll be our little secret.

She winks at him, takes the glass, and goes to drink.

REGAN: Cheers.

GLOUCESTER: Now now now, hold your horses. Slow down. If I'm going to let you at my Nebbiolo, you've got to do it properly.

REGAN: Very well, my lord. I'm at your service.

GLOUCESTER: When tasting wine, you must first breathe it in. Go on. Take a good, long whiff.

She does.

What do you smell?

REGAN: Uh . . . fruit?

GLOUCESTER: Be more specific.

REGAN: . . . grapes?

GLOUCESTER: I do hope so!

REGAN: Oh. Right. Sorry.

GLOUCESTER: Go on. Again.

REGAN: . . . cherries, maybe?

GLOUCESTER: Good girl. Yes.

REGAN: And some sort of flower?

GLOUCESTER: Beautiful. Now, take a sip and swirl it around your mouth. Let it coat your tongue and your teeth and your gums. Now swallow.

REGAN: Whoa.

GLOUCESTER: Yes?

REGAN: There's a different taste after you swallow. Like earth. Or wood.

GLOUCESTER: Well done. With every sip you can taste the soil in which the grapes were grown, the barrel in which the wine was aged, the very sun, even, that cultivated the sugars.

REGAN: Amazing.

GLOUCESTER: Take another sip. Close your eyes this time.

She does.
He kisses her.

REGAN: Whoa . . . whoa . . .

GLOUCESTER: It's all right.

REGAN: But I . . . but . . .

GLOUCESTER: Don't worry.

REGAN: I . . .

GLOUCESTER: Pleasure is the same thing as wine.

REGAN: I should . . .

GLOUCESTER: One has to be taught how to enjoy the good stuff.

He kisses her again.
She pushes him away.

REGAN: No. No, I—

GLOUCESTER: You have an appetite, my dear.

REGAN: What's happening?

GLOUCESTER: You must cultivate that hunger.

REGAN: I have to go—

GLOUCESTER: You don't have to be ashamed of feeling excited.

REGAN: What?

GLOUCESTER: It's startling, at first.

REGAN: But—

GLOUCESTER: And you've been sheltered from the world.

REGAN: I—

GLOUCESTER: Most girls your age—

REGAN: Stop.

GLOUCESTER: Trust me.

REGAN: I said stop!

She pushes him away.
She struggles to pull herself together.

GLOUCESTER: It'll get old quickly, you know. The act.

REGAN: What act?

GLOUCESTER: The come hither, leave me alone act. I'm a good guy. I'm a friend. But most men, most men won't put up with that.

REGAN: What are you talking about?

GLOUCESTER: Oh, come on! Own it, at least. Own it. You can't parade around like you did tonight, flaunting your sex this way and that and not expect to attract attention.

REGAN: I wasn't trying to—

GLOUCESTER: You can't bat your eyes and shake your hips and pretend you don't know what that means.

REGAN: But I wasn't—

GLOUCESTER: You can't put it all out there and not expect men to react.

REGAN: But I didn't do anything—

GLOUCESTER: I saw the way you walked in here.

REGAN: I . . .

GLOUCESTER: There was nothing modest about it.

REGAN: I . . .

GLOUCESTER: You knew what you were looking for.

REGAN: I didn't want . . .

GLOUCESTER: Didn't want what?

He takes her hand and places it on his erect penis.

This.

She freezes.

This is what you've done to me.
Let's see what I've done to you.

He raises her skirts.
Blackout.

Scene 4

LEAR's bedchamber.
He is very drunk.
LEAR sits on the bed. The OLD WOMAN *crouches on a stool in front of him, rubbing his feet.*

OLD WOMAN: So there's this general riding home from the war when his horse stumbles and suddenly goes lame.

LEAR: *(pleasure at the foot rub)* Ohhhhh.

OLD WOMAN: A young soldier hops off his own horse and runs to the general. "General," he says, "has your horse gone lame?" The general hands the boy the reigns of the lame horse and says, "Has *my* horse gone lame?! No, soldier. *Yours* has."

LEAR: Hahah ha ha!

OLD WOMAN: Awww, you've worn out your dancing feet this evening, you poor dear. These bunions aren't getting any smaller.

LEAR: Is that why it's taking them so long to get back?

OLD WOMAN: Who's that?

LEAR: My soldiers. Have their horses gone lame?

OLD WOMAN: Oh, but your soldiers have all returned, Your Majesty.

LEAR: Are you sure?

OLD WOMAN: Don't you hear them?

LEAR: Yes . . .
Yes . . .
Howling in the wind.
Howl. Howl. Howl. Howl.

GONERIL enters.
She is stunned momentarily at the sight of the OLD WOMAN.

GONERIL: What are you doing in here?

OLD WOMAN: Just seeing His Majesty through the after hours, my lady.

GONERIL: What are you wearing?

OLD WOMAN: An old frock your father asks me to put on now and again.

GONERIL: That was my mother's dress.

OLD WOMAN: Ah, yes, I suspected as much, but didn't dare ask.

GONERIL: Take it off.

OLD WOMAN: It does please your father for me to wear it.

GONERIL: Take it off.

OLD WOMAN: Brings him comfort.

GONERIL: Now.

OLD WOMAN: Right away, my lady. Although I will confess, I'm wearing very little underneath.

GONERIL: What?

OLD WOMAN: This fabric is much softer than my undergarments, you see, so I—

GONERIL: Leave us.

OLD WOMAN: You must forgive an old woman for—

GONERIL: Now.

> The OLD WOMAN *exits.*
> LEAR *looks for something on the floor.*

Oh, Father, what are you doing with that old fool?

LEAR: Have you heard the one about the priest?

GONERIL: Off the floor, now.

LEAR: A priest saw a virgin in the . . . no . . . no that's not it . . .

GONERIL: What are you looking for?

LEAR: My slippers. My feet. My slippers.

GONERIL: Into bed now, Father.

LEAR: I can't see a thing in the dark.

GONERIL: Into bed and I'll find them.

LEAR: Sewed them herself. Just for me. I've worn them out, really— they're coming apart at the seams. But the only time I feel like myself is when I put my feet in those slippers.

GONERIL: And what would Mother say if she saw you crawling around on the floor.

She helps him up.

LEAR: Cordelia looks just like her.

GONERIL: I know.

LEAR: Spitting image, don't you think.

GONERIL: Yes, Father.

LEAR: Not you.

GONERIL: No, not me.

LEAR: You're a bit mean-looking.

GONERIL: I probably get that from you.

LEAR: Your mother'd be ashamed of me.

GONERIL: No, she wouldn't.

LEAR: Couldn't stand to see me drunk. Not that she ever nagged, but I knew she disapproved, so moderation seemed—

He vomits into a chamber pot.

GONERIL: It's all right, Father. Better out than in.

LEAR: It's just men. You know, men. We don't mean to get unhinged. Need women to keep us on track. We say we don't but that's the truth of it.

GONERIL finds the slippers.

GONERIL: Here they are.

LEAR: My slippers.

GONERIL: Lie down, now.

LEAR: (*hearing something*) What's that?

GONERIL: Please, Father—

LEAR: Listen.

> *They listen.*
> *Wind.*

Open the window.

GONERIL: You'll catch your death.

LEAR: Let them in.

GONERIL: Who?

LEAR: Crying, they're crying.

GONERIL: Calm down.

LEAR: They're bleeding, they're dying out there.
I need to let them in . . .
Let them in!

GONERIL: Father—

LEAR: They're cursing me, do you hear?
Howling curses into the night.

GONERIL: It's the wind, Father. Only the wind.

EDMUND is out in the corridor, looking for GONERIL.

EDMUND: Goneril? Goneril?

GONERIL: Please, Father, get back into bed.

He allows her to guide him.

EDMUND: Goneril?

GONERIL goes to the door.

GONERIL: What are you doing up here?

EDMUND: It's Regan—she's gone.

LEAR: Gone where?

GONERIL: Nowhere, Father.

EDMUND: I saw her. In the corridor. She looked . . . I called out to her, but she ignored me. I went to her, but she pushed me away. I thought she was joking, so I tried again and she . . .

GONERIL: She what?

EDMUND: Punched me in the face.

GONERIL: How much wine did she drink tonight?

EDMUND: I lost track.

GONERIL: Where is she now?

EDMUND: That's the thing. She ran out into the storm.

GONERIL: Of course she did. I'm sure she made a complete spectacle of herself tonight but that wasn't enough. Now she wants us to chase her out into the storm.

EDMUND: No . . . no, that wasn't it. Something happened, something's wrong.

LEAR: What's wrong?

GONERIL: All right, give me a minute and I'll figure out what to do.

EDMUND exits.

LEAR: What's wrong?

GONERIL: Nothing. Just—Regan.

LEAR: Ah, Regan. She makes me feel young.

GONERIL: I'm sure she does.

LEAR: Do you know what your problem is?

GONERIL: I need you to stay in bed.

LEAR: You take it all so seriously.

GONERIL: That's enough.

LEAR: You're too harsh. Banishing that poor maid.

GONERIL: But . . . but that's what you wanted me to do.

LEAR: You've got to lighten up a bit.

GONERIL: I chose principle over sentiment, law over friendship, calculated action over feeling.

LEAR: And you came off like a bitch.

Beat.

GONERIL: Good night, Father.

He grabs onto her.

LEAR: Don't go, don't leave me.

GONERIL: I have to find Regan.

LEAR: Stay. Please, stay.

GONERIL: She's out in the storm.

LEAR: Tell me you love me.

GONERIL: Not tonight, Father.

LEAR: Tell me how much you love me.

GONERIL: Let me go.

LEAR: Fine! Leave me then! Leave me alone like she left me alone with nothing but lost slippers. No one to talk to, no one to listen. No one to calm the racing, racing, racing— Only pain! Regret!

GONERIL: I love you more than word can wield the matter.

He listens.

Dearer than eyesight, space, and liberty.

LEAR: Yes . . .

GONERIL: Beyond what can be valued, rich or rare,
No less than life, with grace, health, beauty, honour;
As much as child e'er loved, or father found;
A love that makes breath poor and speech unable.
Beyond all manner of so much I love you.

> *He is asleep.*
> *Thunder.*
> *Lightning.*
> *Rain.*

Scene 5

> *Out in the storm.*
> REGAN *first.*
> *Then* GONERIL.
> *Finally,* CORDELIA *in her window.*

REGAN: Blow, winds, and crack your cheeks. Rage, tear,
Drench me through; wash away the mem'ry of
His eyes, which turned me into something raw,
A piece of bloody meat to be devoured.
Pour, rain, teem. Drown the breath that fluttered in
My chest and dizzied me to pause in th'heat.
I longed to run, but muscles froze in place.
I longed to scream, but sound choked in my throat.
I longed to kick and scratch and fight him off,
But I just stood there as he licked me bare.

GONERIL: Rumble thy bellyful! Spit fire, spout rain!
Nor rain, wind, thunder, fire are my father.
I never treated you to loyalty,

Nor watched you scorn my every bold attempt
To prove my actions worthy of your love.
You never promised me succession, then
Suspended me in constant state of waiting.
You never with my dowry gifted land
And held it back upon my wedding day.
You never guaranteed a father's love
Then left me begging to receive it.

Growl, thunder. Roar over the voice in my head saying:

GONERIL & REGAN: This is what you asked for.
This is all your fault.
This is what you deserve.

GONERIL: Blow, winds, blow. Crack your fiery whip
Across the sky and thunder your anger
With a force I cannot wield.

REGAN: Belch your buckets of angry tears
And wash away my strained attempts at self-pity.

> *Lights up on* CORDELIA *in her window.*
> *She's not smiling.*

GONERIL: Ensnarl my hair.

REGAN: Tear off these woman's weeds.

GONERIL: Engorge my skirts.

REGAN: Bedim these baiting eyes.

GONERIL: Now scour from my brow this calm facade.

REGAN: And smear these flushèd cheeks with filthy soil.

GONERIL: Release me from attentive, poised remarks.

REGAN: Eviscerate the flame that burned in me.

GONERIL: Extinguish my accommodating gaze.

REGAN: Regan, I nothing am.

GONERIL: Goneril, I will no more be.

> *The sky blazes with thunder, rain, and lightning.*
> CORDELIA*'s song blasts into the night—punk rock, heavy metal.*
> *This can be incorporated into the sound design or she can sing:*

CORDELIA: My hands are soft, thy limbs are weary,
I will comfort thee.
My voice is clear, thine eyes are bleary,
I will comfort thee.
I will comfort thee
I will . . .

> *Blackout.*

Act 4

Scene 1

The storm.
OLENA appears dressed in men's clothing.

OSWALD: I knew she was being forced to choose:
power or comfort, greatness or loyalty, kingdom or love.
When Goneril looked at me in that throne room
I understood what she desired: both.
Kneel and give me both, she said with her eyes.
But I couldn't bring myself to do it.

Goneril has always said that any child of hers would be mine.
And yet, when I learned she was with child,
I felt the jealousy of a cuckolded husband.
Except, of course, I am no husband.
Not in shape or contract.
In promise only.
And what is a promise when the world begins to change?
What is love if it can only thrive in secrecy?

So, I forced Goneril to choose.
And choose, she did.
Now, I must go on.

To travel safely, I've traded my skirts and corset
for a jacket and breeches.

Instant relief.
My legs can stretch to the full gait of my stride,
my breath can fill my lungs,
and my voice has lowered to its natural pitch.
With the past behind me, I am free
to move through the world unencumbered.
And yet, the world, it seems, would have it otherwise.
In the bark of this tree, I see Goneril's smile.
In the wind that now presses against me,
I feel her body pressed against mine.
I can almost smell my lover's skin on the back of the rain,
the taste of her, even . . .

Would that the pain she has caused me
be enough to drive her image from my mind.
But like a dog craving kindness from his cruel master,
my heart returns for the next inevitable beating.
It appears that no amount of bitterness can make me walk away.

> GONERIL *appears in the distance.*

Even now, my eyes play tricks on me.

GONERIL: Regan!

OSWALD: Is that Goneril, in the distance? Stumbling through rain and fog?

GONERIL: Regan!

OSWALD: Maybe I should hide myself.

Scene 2

GONERIL: Hey, there! Young man!

OSWALD: My lady?

GONERIL: Have you seen a woman?

OSWALD: Other than you?

GONERIL: A reckless woman. Wild. Running, likely running.

OSWALD: I haven't, my lady, I'm sorry.
But you should get back to the palace.

GONERIL: The palace? Who are you? Do you know me?

OSWALD: Everyone knows you, my lady.
My name is . . . Oswald.

GONERIL: Oswald?

OSWALD: Second son to the Lord of Leicester. With respect, you shouldn't be out on a night like this. You must seek shelter.

GONERIL: Shelter! I'm not the one who needs shelter.

OSWALD: My lady?

GONERIL: I have been sheltered all of my life, but look.

OSWALD: Where?

GONERIL: Across the field at the edge of the forest.

OSWALD: You mean that row of abandoned cottages?

GONERIL: Not abandoned, no, look closer, Oswald.
See the men trying to prop up their thatched roofs?

OSWALD: Yes.

GONERIL: Their families are huddled inside with no fire to keep out the cold.
No warm blankets, no food to fill their starving bellies.

OSWALD: Come out of the rain, my lady.

GONERIL: They live like this day in and day out.
Assaulted by the elements,
dying from exposure, starvation, illness,
and what have I done about it?

OSWALD: I'm sure you've tried to help.

GONERIL: You're wrong. I haven't.
I've been playing chess and speaking French
and galloping past their suffering with a rifle slung over my shoulder.
And all for what?

OSWALD: So you could help them as their future queen.

GONERIL: Queen?! Ha! I will never be Queen.

OSWALD: From what I hear, my lady, you were born to be a ruler.

GONERIL: And what is a ruler, Oswald?
Is it someone who stands on a mountain of history?
Or one who looks to the stars for the future?
Is it the king who secures and defends his borders?

Or the one who goes beyond, to invade and expand?
Does a ruler enlighten or advance? Empower or command?
Does a ruler resemble his people?
Or can you honestly say you would follow a ruler that looks
like me?

OSWALD: Surely, it is a leader's values that matter most.

GONERIL: Well, I have spent my life trying to embody regal values
like intelligence, strength, and honour.
I can speak with authority on any number of subjects,
exchange pointed witticisms over dinner,
or be cutthroat in a negotiation.
And I have delighted at the delight men take
at seeing me effortlessly navigate a man's world.
"Look at Goneril," they say, amazed,
"she isn't like other women;
she can keep up with the boys;
she's almost one of us."
Except that I am not.

Another value tugs at my heart,
begging to be released from the cage I've locked it in.

OSWALD: Compassion?

GONERIL: Yes. Yes, compassion.

OSWALD: But why lock it away?
Is compassion not a strength?

GONERIL: For a woman, yes, in the home.
Compassion involves the drying of tears,
and endless, unacknowledged hours of caring for other people.
To live with compassion is to subjugate the self,
to promote the well-being of others.

OSWALD: You are trembling, my lady.

GONERIL: Don't you see?
If I were to embody compassion, I would surely erase myself.
Who would kneel to an invisible queen?

OSWALD: Let's get you out of the cold.

GONERIL: I need to find my sister.

GONERIL starts to exit.

OSWALD: But, my lady—

GONERIL: Regan!!!!
Regan!!!

Scene 3

CORDELIA is leaving the palace with a packed bag.

OLD WOMAN: So you're off then, are you.

CORDELIA: I . . .

OLD WOMAN: Packed everything you need?

CORDELIA: Don't try to stop me.

OLD WOMAN: I wouldn't dream of it.

CORDELIA: I'm leaving.

OLD WOMAN: I can see that.

CORDELIA: And I'm never coming back.

OLD WOMAN: Can't say I'm not sad to see you go, but I understand completely.

CORDELIA: You do?

OLD WOMAN: Absolutely.

CORDELIA: Good.

OLD WOMAN: Take care to bundle up.

CORDELIA: Yes.

OLD WOMAN: That storm is quite fierce.

CORDELIA: Yes.

OLD WOMAN: Farewell.

CORDELIA turns to leave, then turns back.

CORDELIA: I'm a liar, you know.

OLD WOMAN: Ah.

CORDELIA: And I always have been.

OLD WOMAN: Huh.

CORDELIA: I'm . . . I'm not who I appear to be.

OLD WOMAN: Most people aren't, my lady.

CORDELIA: But my whole . . . everything . . . it's just . . . I am not kind-hearted. I'm not sweet or loving and I don't always see the good in other people. I'm jealous. And I'm just so angry. And I think horrible thoughts sometimes but I never let them out—I can't let them out because I have to keep smiling.

OLD WOMAN: What would happen if you stopped?

CORDELIA: Everything would fall apart.

OLD WOMAN: What would?

CORDELIA: My father, my sisters, the kingdom.

OLD WOMAN: That's a lot riding on a young woman's smile.

CORDELIA: You're making fun of me.

OLD WOMAN: Not at all. You're upset.

CORDELIA: It's not just that.

OLD WOMAN: You feel compelled to keep the peace.

CORDELIA: My sisters think I'm just this simple little child, only there to entertain, like I don't understand anything complicated. But really, I'm the only one who sees it. Really sees it.

OLD WOMAN: What's that?

CORDELIA: The pain. So much pain. In everyone. It floods into me because I welcome it to share the burden, but I couldn't hold it any longer . . . I've done something bad.

OLD WOMAN: Well, that was bound to happen.

CORDELIA: And then I lied about it.

OLD WOMAN: Ah, I see. A lie is like a rotting tooth: the pain gets worse the longer you ignore it.

CORDELIA: What should I do?

OLD WOMAN: Best to yank it out as soon as possible.

CORDELIA: I don't know if I can.

OLD WOMAN: Let's get you up to bed, my lady, and talk about it in the morning.

CORDELIA: But what about the tooth?

OLD WOMAN: We'll yank it out after a good night's sleep.

CORDELIA: But I can't bear this feeling any longer.

OLD WOMAN: Lady Cordelia—

CORDELIA: My sisters ran out in the storm.

OLD WOMAN: Nonsense.

CORDELIA: I've got to find them.

OLD WOMAN: My lady—

CORDELIA: Right now!

CORDELIA runs off into the storm.

OLD WOMAN: Gods give me strength!

The OLD WOMAN chases after CORDELIA.

Scene 4

GONERIL and OSWALD enter the playhouse.
GONERIL is exhausted.

GONERIL: Regan? Regan?

OSWALD: What is this place?

GONERIL: Oh, that smell. It smells the same.

OSWALD: Some sort of playhouse?

GONERIL: My sister and I spent days out here after our mother died. Weeks, even . . . We'd act out these scenes. (*finding a play crown*) My crown. I'd be Queen . . . and Regan would try to usurp me . . . we had this knife . . . Regan . . .

OSWALD: Maybe you should sit down.

GONERIL swoons and OSWALD catches her.
He helps her sit down.

Easy now, I've got you. Just sit. Breathe.

GONERIL: Olena?

OSWALD: That's not my name.

GONERIL: Olena, it's you.

OSWALD: No.

GONERIL: It's you, you've come back—I'm so sorry.

OSWALD: I am Oswald, second son to the Lord of Leicester. I'll stay with you until you're safe, but then I will go.

GONERIL: No, please, no. You were right. All along. You were right. This is too much. I've sacrificed too much. I'm going to stop.

OSWALD: Stop what?

GONERIL: Trying to become what I am not. We'll go home. I'll have this child. Our child. We'll be together. Simply. Just us.

OSWALD: That won't be enough for you.

GONERIL: But I can see it now. I can see myself rocking our baby while you, you stoke the fire.

OSWALD: Goneril—

GONERIL: Please. I know you can see it too.

OSWALD: What I can or cannot see has never been the issue.

CORDELIA bursts in followed by the OLD WOMAN.

CORDELIA: I'm sorry.

GONERIL: Cordelia?

CORDELIA: I'm sorry, Goneril.

GONERIL: What are you doing out here?

CORDELIA: Did you find Regan?

GONERIL: *(to the OLD WOMAN)* She's drenched. Why didn't you stop her?

OLD WOMAN: Took everything I had to keep up with her, my lady.

CORDELIA: I'm so sorry.

GONERIL: What have I told you about apologizing.

CORDELIA: But I lied.

GONERIL: (*to the* OLD WOMAN) Get her out of those wet clothes.

CORDELIA: You aren't listening to me.

GONERIL: Calm down, Cordelia.

CORDELIA: I lied about the music box.

GONERIL: That's all over now.

CORDELIA: I'm the one who hid it.

> *Beat.*

I'm the one who put it in Olena's room.

GONERIL: But . . . why?

CORDELIA: I wanted to hurt you.

GONERIL: I've done nothing but care for you since the day you were born.

CORDELIA: You barely even look at me.

GONERIL: What are you talking about?

CORDELIA: Or when you do, you look through me, or tell me to never change because I'm good and honest like a child, like a doll, like life is so easy for me.

GONERIL: Well, you're always smiling / so I thought—

CORDELIA: This smile is a lie.
Just a way to make sure that people love me.

GONERIL: I've always loved you unconditionally.

CORDELIA: No. No. You love Regan unconditionally. The two of you are bound to one another.

GONERIL: We're at each other's throats.

CORDELIA: But it's like there's an invisible band between you and the harder you pull away from one another, the more forcefully you're snapped back together.

You both had our mother. You know what she smelled like. What she sang like. What it felt like when she was braiding your hair or stroking your back or scolding you, even, for hiding a music box.

GONERIL: You never ask about her.

CORDELIA: Because I can't. No one ever talks about her. It's like she didn't even exist. It's like a secret you're keeping from me, and I want to ask you about her—I want to ask all the time but I don't because I know it hurts too much and it's worse because I look like her, because I'm the reason she's dead.

> *REGAN is heard from the shadows.*
> *Throughout the next scene she plays out court scenes as in the game in Act One.*
> *She plays all characters in her fantasy.*

REGAN: Order!

OSWALD: Who's there?

REGAN: Order in the court!

GONERIL: Regan? I've been looking all over for you.

REGAN: Next case!
- Here we have a wretched creature.
A spider. A hog. A worm. A bitch in heat.
A beast governed by unquenchable desire.
Of what does this woman stand accused?
The list is endless, Your Honour, but we'll start with jealousy.
Of whom is this woman jealous?
Her impressive older sister.

GONERIL: I don't know what you're trying to prove here, but—

REGAN: This woman is guilty of so many things, Your Honour.

GONERIL: Stop it, Regan.

REGAN: I will not stop until this woman has been prosecuted for her crimes.

GONERIL: Regan—

REGAN pulls out an old knife.

OSWALD: Stand back.

REGAN: This woman must stand trial.

OSWALD: Put the knife down.

GONERIL: It's all right.

REGAN: She must be prosecuted for her crimes.

Beat.

     Do it!

GONERIL: Of what does this woman stand accused?

REGAN: Defiance.

GONERIL: Defiance of what?

REGAN: Everything.
     Let it please the court that this woman felt betrayed
     when her sister abandoned her.

GONERIL: Does this woman imagine her sister should not have
married?

REGAN: Objection!

GONERIL: What did you want me to do? Hole up with you in this
playhouse and imagine a life rather than live one?

REGAN: Order in the court.
     The only way this woman could keep the loneliness
     at bay was to push up against the limits, the con-
     straints, the rules.
     And broken rules lead to broken illusions.

GONERIL: What illusions?

REGAN: That our bodies are made of metal.
           That a blow will never land,
           a sword will never pierce.
           We believe the invisible weapons we wield—
           the jokes, the tears, the words of reproach—
           are enough to defend these vile frames of ours.
           These weak muscles.
           These hidden places.
           But they're not.
           They're not.

GONERIL: What happened tonight?

REGAN: I hereby charge this woman with naïveté.

GONERIL: Where did her naïveté lead?

REGAN: Down the steps.

GONERIL: And then?

REGAN: Into the cellar.

GONERIL: And then?

REGAN: Against a cold wall.

GONERIL: And then?

REGAN: Out of herself.

GONERIL: Regan . . .

    REGAN sees GONERIL as though for the first time.

REGAN: Why did you make me push so hard?

I would have stayed with you.

Now I've gone and torn myself apart.

Chunks of me are hanging by a thread.

GONERIL: I've got you.

REGAN: I'll never piece them back together.

GONERIL: I've got you, it's okay.

REGAN: Never never never never.

> *GONERIL* holds *REGAN.*

GONERIL: This whole thing.
This whole world is against us.
Either we tiptoe through it, smiling so as not to disrupt anything,
or we push against it, knowing we'll be pushed back,
or we disguise ourselves within it,
trying to convince one another that it also belongs to us.
But it doesn't.
This world wasn't built for us.
It's full of violence and shame and secrets.
Full of starving people and abandoned people,
dead people waiting for release.

I am so tired of trying to follow these invisible rules,
of transforming myself into the shape of what's expected.

CORDELIA: But what else can we do?

GONERIL: We can take it apart.

> *Beat.*

We're going to burn that pile of bodies.

CORDELIA: The soldiers? But . . . we can't.

GONERIL: Why not?

CORDELIA: Kent brought those men home to give them a proper burial.

GONERIL: And instead those bodies are defiled by the elements.

CORDELIA: Father is planning a ceremony.

GONERIL: What ceremony?! There is no ceremony. Just waiting, endless waiting for Father to honour those who deserve to be honoured. We can't stand by any longer, watching the decay.

OSWALD: It's been pouring all night. We couldn't even make a spark.

OLD WOMAN: Rained goats and chickens the night before my mother was burned at the stake.

OSWALD: I'm sorry, what?

OLD WOMAN: She got caught singing in her language over a pot of stew. Witches were in season back then. Public burnings quell peasant revolts, or that was the thinking at the time. Now executioners didn't like to postpone a burning so before sunrise on the day of my mother's execution, they told me and my sister to coat the pyre in pig fat. "Be thorough," they said. "Don't want your mother to suffer more than she has to." We did our best and it worked a charm. Quite the blaze.

CORDELIA: That's awful.

OLD WOMAN: It's all right, pup. I've seen a lot of fires since then.

GONERIL: And where exactly would we find that much pig fat?

OLD WOMAN: I got a couple of barrels behind the kitchen ready for making soap.

REGAN: Father will be pissed.

GONERIL: Let him be pissed. Those souls need to be honoured. They need to be released.

Scene 5

GONERIL, REGAN, CORDELIA, OSWALD, and the OLD WOMAN stand
before a massive pile of burning corpses.
There is space in the gaps in the text.

REGAN: are they glad, do you think?

GONERIL: who?

REGAN: the men
their souls

CORDELIA: i think so

OSWALD: so do i

GONERIL: me too

OLD WOMAN: dead don't like to linger

OLD WOMAN: smells of mortality

GONERIL: of possibility

REGAN: change

OSWALD: warning

CORDELIA: release
i feel my blood

REGAN: i know what you mean

CORDELIA: my heartbeat

REGAN: yes

CORDELIA: my breath

GONERIL: look up
the clouds have cleared

GONERIL: remember sitting in front of the fire while mother braided our hair?

REGAN: she had big hands
strong hands

GONERIL: (*to* CORDELIA) regan could never sit still

CORDELIA: surpise surprise

REGAN: i only squirmed so she'd tell us stories

CORDELIA: what kind of stories?

GONERIL: about her people
her home

CORDELIA: yes?

GONERIL: a place far from here where title and land
are passed from mother to daughter

REGAN: imagine that

GONERIL: will you forgive me?

OSWALD: don't think i can stop myself

GONERIL: i'm sorry

OSWALD: i know

GONERIL: i like the breeches

OSWALD: yeah?

GONERIL: yeah

OSWALD: started out as a disguise
but
i don't know
feels like the skirts were the real disguise

GONERIL: what do you mean?

OSWALD: this is me

GONERIL: yes
this is you

OSWALD: you look tired

GONERIL: so do you

OSWALD: drained, though
doesn't she?

REGAN: yes
she does

CORDELIA: is something wrong?

REGAN: are you okay?

GONERIL: (*realizing*) i . . .

GONERIL puts her hand under her clothing.
When she brings it out, it's covered in blood.

it's . . . leaving me

CORDELIA: oh no

REGAN: maybe not

OSWALD: you should sit

GONERIL: no

OSWALD: i'll find a midwife

GONERIL: no

REGAN: you need some cloth

GONERIL: don't touch me

OSWALD: goneril

GONERIL: don't touch me!

OLD WOMAN: i buried three before they came
another two, just after
pain of it still beats through me without warning
it doesn't go away
you just add it to the day-to-day

GONERIL: i don't want to accumulate pain

OLD WOMAN: ah, but pain can be a comfort

GONERIL: how's that?

OLD WOMAN: it means you've not forgotten

GONERIL: i thought i needed to wait for . . .

the timing wasn't . . .

i didn't want . . .

but then . . .

i fell in love with . . .

i was so . . .

but now . . .

i feel . . .

i feel . . .

i feel . . .

REGAN: yes
feel

GONERIL: i feel . . . weak

OSWALD: yes
be weak

GONERIL: needy

OLD WOMAN: yes
be needy

REGAN: be angry

OLD WOMAN: be numb

OSWALD: be desperate

CORDELIA: be lonely

REGAN: be scared

OLD WOMAN: invisible

CORDELIA: nothing

OSWALD: anything

REGAN: everything
everything
and more

> *CORDELIA sings.*
> *Simply. Slowly. Quietly.*
> *They all listen.*

CORDELIA: My hands are soft, thy limbs are weary,
I will comfort thee.
My voice is clear, thine eyes are bleary,
I will comfort thee.
I will foresee thy every need,
Before it weighs upon thee.
Thy soul is tired, but I am cheery,
I will comfort thee.

Act 5

Scene 1

Morning.
The next day.
GLOUCESTER *enters with his bag.*

GLOUCESTER: Are the trunks all packed?

EDMUND: We're leaving now?

GLOUCESTER: Best to get an early start.

EDMUND: Before breakfast?

GLOUCESTER: Edgar comes home today and I want to make certain everything's ready for his return.

EDMUND: All hail the legitimate son!

GLOUCESTER: Don't be bitter, my boy, it doesn't suit you.

EDMUND: I'm not . . . bitter. It's just—after the fire last night, shouldn't we make sure everyone's all right before we go.

GLOUCESTER: I'm sure everyone's fine.

EDMUND: We should at least say a proper goodbye.

GLOUCESTER: Let's just sneak out before anyone wakes.

EDMUND: Sneak? Why would we . . . (*realizing*) Oh no. You didn't . . .

> GLOUCESTER *shrugs an admission.*

Not again, Father.

GLOUCESTER: Thank Apollo for bastards, that's all I have to say. I wouldn't trade you for five more legitimate sons.

EDMUND: Why do you do this?

GLOUCESTER: (*his head aches*) Ohhhhh my head. Find my compound, will you?

> *He passes* EDMUND *his bag.*
> EDMUND *looks for his father's medicine.*

EDMUND: Well sit down, drink some water.

GLOUCESTER: Bastards are acquainted with their father's sins so they cannot be disillusioned by them.

EDMUND: Unlike you, I am capable of living a moral life.

GLOUCESTER: All I'm saying is that you can stand to see the ugly side of a man and not dismiss his entire character. Edgar, on the other hand, is somewhat more fragile.

EDMUND: That's an understatement.

GLOUCESTER: He doesn't have the constitution to witness ugliness.

EDMUND: Well, we all have our faults.

GLOUCESTER: Precisely my meaning. You have a malleable sense of morality, so I don't feel shame in revealing my whole self to you. Even after one of my . . . episodes.

EDMUND: What happened?

GLOUCESTER: Kent says if the maids don't know by now to steer clear of me when I'm drunk, they need to have their heads examined.

EDMUND: You really are a bit of a pervert, Father.

GLOUCESTER: Ha! Haha ha ha ha! (*his head aches*) Ohhhhh—

EDMUND: (*giving him the medicine*) Here you are.

GLOUCESTER: That second-last bottle was one too many!

GLOUCESTER takes his medicine.

EDMUND: So . . . which one?

GLOUCESTER: What's that?

EDMUND: Which maid did you take liberties with last night?

GLOUCESTER: Why on earth would you need to know that?

EDMUND: In case there are repercussions.

GLOUCESTER: What repercussions?

EDMUND: Sometimes there are repercussions. You just don't know about them because I'm the one who sorts it out.

GLOUCESTER: You overexaggerate.

EDMUND: Round bellies, vengeful brothers, an angry king.

GLOUCESTER: King? What do you mean?

EDMUND: This is Lear's palace, Father. I can't imagine he'd be too pleased to know you've been ravishing his maids.

GLOUCESTER: That girl was craving attention.

EDMUND: From you?

GLOUCESTER: From anyone who would look her way. I tell you, she was very much enthralled by the attention I paid her, despite a certain hesitancy out of the gates.

EDMUND: So she resisted.

GLOUCESTER: All women say no.

EDMUND: Then you should leave all women alone.

GLOUCESTER: Out of propriety, only.

EDMUND: Or because they don't want you touching them.

GLOUCESTER: All women are centaurs below the waist, you know that. No matter how much they protest. No matter who their fathers are.

EDMUND: Ah ha: repercussions.

GLOUCESTER: In the morning light I suppose I can see that there was a certain . . . disrespect to it all. That maybe I . . . took things too far, or . . . it's hard to remember . . . there are pieces missing, holes in my memory . . .

She won't tell him, will she?

EDMUND: Her father? How should I know?

GLOUCESTER: You're . . . well . . . friends.

EDMUND: What?

GLOUCESTER: Maybe you could have a word with her.

EDMUND: No . . .

GLOUCESTER: Make sure she's not feeling too embarrassed.

EDMUND: No no no / no . . .

GLOUCESTER: Some women regret their enthusiasm the next day and I wouldn't want the king to get word of—

EDMUND: You vile, sick, disgusting old man!

GLOUCESTER: Edmund!

EDMUND: You infected germ!

GLOUCESTER: How dare you speak to me like that.

EDMUND: How dare I?

GLOUCESTER: Calm down, now, you've seen what she's like. There's one in every family, bursting with lust.

EDMUND: And it's you, Father! You're the one!

GLOUCESTER: Shhhh. Do you want to wake the palace?!

EDMUND: Maybe we should. Get it all out in the open. Tell everyone what you've done.

GLOUCESTER: Is that what Regan would want?

EDMUND: Don't you dare speak her name.

Beat.
EDGAR *appears in the doorway.*

EDGAR: Bonjour, Papa!

GLOUCESTER: Edgar? Edgar, my boy, is that you?

EDGAR: I was told I'd find the two of you here.

GLOUCESTER: You're back!

EDGAR: And just in time to rescue the both of you from a very tense conversation.

GLOUCESTER: Yes . . . yes, well, not so tense.
We were merely talking about . . .

EDMUND: Astronomy.

EDGAR: Well, now, that's precisely my area of expertise.

EDMUND: You don't say.

EDGAR: Ah. Haha, mon frère. I've missed your sense of humour.

GLOUCESTER: But I had thought you'd return directly to our estate.

EDGAR: I did, but when I realized you were here, I came to find you. The most extraordinary thing is going to happen this afternoon and I couldn't bear for you to miss it.

GLOUCESTER: Oh?

EDGAR: A total eclipse of the sun.

GLOUCESTER: Fascinating.

EDGAR: If my calculations are correct, we will find ourselves in the direct path of the umbra.

GLOUCESTER: Did you hear that, Edmund?

EDMUND: Thrilling.

EDGAR: Imagine, the moon's dark shadow rushing across the landscape as the disc of the sun diminishes into a crescent. Then, finally, as the moon assumes its position directly in front of the sun, we will be plunged into total darkness.

EDMUND: Sounds like we might have missed it if you weren't here to point it out.

EDGAR: Ha ha.

GLOUCESTER: If we set out now, we could see it from home.

EDGAR: Oh, nonsense, I've already set up my telescope in the courtyard. Let's hope the smoke fully clears by this afternoon.

> EDGAR *and* GLOUCESTER *start to exit.*

Of course, one must never look directly at a solar eclipse, so I have devised a semi-transparent screen for the lens.

Well, come along, Edmund. We wouldn't want you to miss the show.

Scene 2

GONERIL and LEAR in the throne room.

LEAR: Get out of my sight.

GONERIL: The people are glad, Father.

LEAR: What do you know about the people.

GONERIL: I told Kent to blame the storm.

LEAR: Giving orders now.

GONERIL: Someone has to.

LEAR: Don't talk back to me.

    Beat.

Those soldiers deserved a proper burial.

GONERIL: Months ago.

LEAR: Breakfast!
And how do you think their mothers feel?

GONERIL: Relieved. There was nothing dignified about that pile of corpses. The king of my childhood never would have allowed that spectacle to go on for so long. That king took time to think before he acted and then he acted swiftly. Deftly. With precision.

LEAR: I haven't changed.

GONERIL: No? You're impatient, impulsive. Distracted.

LEAR: You don't know anything.

GONERIL: I know everything. All I've done for the past two months is watch you, day in and day out.

LEAR: Yes, probing me for signs of weakness.

GONERIL: Hoping to glean a bit of wisdom before you throw it all away.

LEAR: Bah!

GONERIL: If you keep heading along this track, it won't be the good years people remember.

LEAR: Stop it.

GONERIL: It will be your selfishness.

LEAR: Stop it.

GONERIL: Your drunkenness.

LEAR: Stop.

GONERIL: Your incompetence.

LEAR: Stop / stop stop stop—

GONERIL: I won't stop. I can't stop, because if I do, our kingdom will fall to ruin. Open your eyes, Father. Trade agreements have collapsed, people are starving, a plague is on the horizon. This kingdom is in need and you are doing everything you can to ignore it. Let me help, Father. Let me lead.

LEAR: You're not ready.

GONERIL: Why not?

LEAR: Just, not ready.

GONERIL: But you've seen me in trade negotiations.

LEAR: It's not the bloody trade agreements.

GONERIL: Then tell me.

LEAR: You don't have the constitution!

Beat.

GONERIL: The constitution. You mean because I'm a woman.

LEAR: That's not—

GONERIL: Now we're getting to it.

LEAR: You are capable of many things.

GONERIL: But sitting on the throne is not one of them.

LEAR: I've been too lenient with you girls. Given you the impression—

GONERIL: You raised me to be strong. Independent. A problem-solver.

LEAR: You are, my dear.

GONERIL: But in the end, you only see me as a member of the weaker sex.

LEAR: Not weaker. Superior, in many ways.

GONERIL: Yes, yes, yes, superior in taking care of the men around me. Superior at raising future kings and decorating a palace.

LEAR: You know I think more highly of you than that.

GONERIL: You build up my confidence, then cut it down. Give me responsibilities, then take them away. Praise me one minute and chastise me the next.

LEAR: And yet, through it all, you've managed to hold your head up high.

GONERIL: Then why are you standing in my way?

LEAR: Because you don't understand the cost.
You can't possibly know the magnitude of the decisions
you will be required to make.
Those men you set fire to last night, they were the cost.
I wasn't even there when they died.
I was here in this room, receiving reports from the front.
How many wounded.
How many lost.
And should we continue?
Should we press on?

How do you answer those questions from a throne room?
My hands are stained with the blood of men who were killed
a hundred leagues from here and I . . .
I can't bear to think of your hands covered in blood.
Your arms, your shoulders, your neck;
I see you standing in a river of blood,
watching it flow around you,
until it sweeps you away.

GONERIL: I am not frightened of blood.

LEAR: You don't know about blood.

GONERIL: Do you honestly think women have no experience
with pain?
We are makers of life and collectors of grief.
I watched Mother succumb to death
even as she was birthing life.
I watched the midwife press on her belly to make the bleeding stop
as the sheets soaked through,
as my baby sister cried.
I held my mother's hand as she died.

LEAR: I didn't know you were in the room.

GONERIL: There may be, on a battlefield in my future,
a sight more horrific,
a pain more wrenching than that which I have already lived,
but I promise you, Father, I will not turn away.
I will not shut my eyes or back down in fear.
I will fight for this kingdom, for its people,
and that fight, it will not break me.

> *Beat.*

LEAR: You're just like her, you know.
Your mother.

GONERIL: I . . .

LEAR: She had this fearlessness, this determination, and once she
fixed her mind on something, that was it. Like me, for example.
Once she decided I was the one . . .

And we were happy. We were. But she could never live in this kingdom as her full self. As a . . . foreigner . . . as an African woman. The things people said to her—to me . . . She remained so steady and strong, forgiving of ignorance, even when I was not. Everyone came to adore her—they couldn't help themselves—still, every now and then, out of the blue a courtier would say . . . the most horrific thing. I can't bear to think of that vitriol directed at you.

GONERIL: I live my life in the face of that vitriol, evading slights, amending misconceptions.

LEAR: It will get worse if you are Queen.
Trust me.
All eyes will be on you.
Examining. Criticizing.

GONERIL: And those eyes will see a Black woman.
A leader with intelligence. Strength. Honour.
One who is not without fault, but who listens to her subjects and makes decisions with compassion.

LEAR: Yes . . .
You really think you're ready to be Queen?

GONERIL: I do.

LEAR: Then . . . so do I.
It's yours.

GONERIL: Really?

LEAR: Really. We'll find a good moment to make the announcement.

GONERIL: Thank you, Father.
I will not let you down.

Scene 3

The throne room.
REGAN enters with EDMUND close behind.

EDMUND: Regan, please—

REGAN: I don't want to talk about it.

EDMUND: But I need to tell you—

REGAN: Please, give me some space.

EDMUND: But I just want to say—

REGAN: What?

EDMUND: I'm sorry. It was my fault. I should have stayed with you, should have made sure you got back upstairs—

REGAN: That wasn't your responsibility.

EDMUND: I should have been there.

REGAN: It's fine.

EDMUND: I feel so bad.

REGAN: This isn't about you.

EDMUND: But I should have warned you.

REGAN: Warned me?

EDMUND: I should have / said something.

REGAN: Wait, you knew?

EDMUND: Only that he sometimes . . . well, when he's drinking—

REGAN: You knew.

EDMUND: No . . . no, I—I mean, I never thought he'd—

REGAN: He's done this before.

EDMUND: Well, yes, but only with—

REGAN: Scullery maids? Kitchen wenches? Well, that's all right then.

EDMUND: I didn't mean—

REGAN: I can't believe you.

EDMUND: Regan—

REGAN: Leave me alone.

EDMUND: Please.

REGAN: Get away from me!

> EDMUND *exits.*
> CORDELIA, OSWALD, *and* GONERIL *enter.*

CORDELIA: You told him we started the fire?

OSWALD: How did he react?

CORDELIA: What else did you say to him?

GONERIL: Regan, there you are.

GONERIL hugs REGAN.

It's going to happen. I'm going to be Queen.

REGAN: What?

GONERIL: We're going to change things. Everything. You're going to be my top advisor. And Cordelia, I'll need you too. We're going to do this together.

CORDELIA: This is it?

GONERIL: Yes. This is it.

OSWALD: I'm glad you'll have your sisters by your side.

GONERIL: And you.

OSWALD: There's no place for me here.

GONERIL: There is. With me.

OSWALD: You know that's impossible.

GONERIL: Now is the moment to make the impossible possible.

A laugh from the men as they approach.
ALBANY, CORNWALL, KENT, and LEAR enter laughing at a joke.
ALBANY sees GONERIL and moves toward her.

ALBANY: There's our little lambkin! I've been looking all over for you.

GONERIL: Albany? But . . . what are you doing here?

ALBANY: Don't get too excited to see your old husband!

CORNWALL: Maybe she doesn't recognize you.

ALBANY: I suppose it has been two whole months!

GONERIL: It's just . . . I didn't expect you back so soon. And at the palace.

ALBANY: Surprise.

He kisses her.

KENT: Daring move, Albany. In front of her father and all!

LEAR: The Duke of Albany laughs in the face of danger. Don't you, son.

ALBANY: I've got to sneak those kisses when I can. You'll see once you get hitched, Kent.

KENT: I'm married to the army for a few more years, but then I'll happily chase my wife around our little cottage.

CORNWALL: Modest aspirations.

KENT: I'm a simple man.

LEAR: But surely you'd miss it.

KENT: The army?

LEAR: The respect. The command. The fame.

KENT: All of that's just for show, though, isn't it. To get the job done. Speaking of which, I should get back to my men.

LEAR: Leaving already?

KENT: We're going to pay our respects to the families of the soldiers who've been laid to rest.

LEAR: Of course, of course.

KENT: But I can't leave without a smile from my ray of sunshine over here. Are you well, Cordelia?

CORDELIA: Yes, my lord.

KENT: It's only—I don't think I've ever seen you without a smile.

CORDELIA: From now on I'll only smile when there's something to smile about.

KENT: I see.

CORDELIA: And I'll never find your departure to be a pleasant thing.

KENT: Fair enough. But you can't even spare just a little one for the road?

Beat.

LEAR: Come on, sweetest. It's just a smile.

CORDELIA: It's never just a smile.

KENT: Well then.

CORDELIA: How about a friendly farewell instead.

KENT: A friendly farewell it is.

GLOUCESTER, EDGAR, and EDMUND *enter.*

EDGAR: Oh, but you can't go yet.

GONERIL: Edgar? You're back too?

All welcome him.

EDGAR: We've all descended on your father at once, I'm afraid. But it's lovely to see you ladies looking so well. Vous êtes vraiment belles.

KENT: Ooo la la! He's come back all fancy!

EDGAR: But, Kent, you really mustn't go until this afternoon or you'll miss the eclipse.

GONERIL: Eclipse?

EDGAR: A total solar eclipse, to be precise. If my calculations are correct, we will find ourselves in the direct path of the umbra.

LEAR: As it seems we all have time to spare before this natural occurrence, let us make room for one more celebration. I have an announcement to make. Although this moment has been a long time coming—some might say too long—I am finally ready to see it through. As you all know, I have been blessed with three extraordinary daughters, each with her own talents. One of those daughters has waited patiently—and sometimes not so patiently—for me to make up my mind. Today, I have. It is with a happy heart that I announce the engagement of my daughter Regan to the Duke of Cornwall.

CORNWALL: And it is with an even happier heart that I will soon be able to call you father.

LEAR: Regan? What say you?

REGAN: I . . .
This is . . .

KENT: Regan, speechless? Now I have seen everything.

REGAN: I am, of course, honoured, my lord. This is . . . news, indeed.

CORNWALL: Pleasant news, I hope.

REGAN: It's hard for me to say having only met you once before.

CORNWALL: I assure you, I am very charming.

REGAN: Of that I have no doubt.
Earl of Gloucester.
What do you think of this match, my lord?

GLOUCESTER: Uhhh . . .

REGAN: As my father's closest advisor, someone he trusts deeply
with all his possessions and affairs, someone I have grown to trust
and admire, I am very curious to hear your thoughts on this match.

GLOUCESTER: The Duke of Cornwall is an honourable man.

LEAR: Are you quite all right, Gloucester?

GLOUCESTER: Yes, Your Majesty.

LEAR: You're red as a tomato.

GLOUCESTER: A little worse for wear after last night.

LEAR: Aren't we all. Well, Regan, what do you say? We're all awaiting your response.

REGAN: Congratulations, Duke of Cornwall. You've got yourself a wife.

Everyone cheers.

Now, perhaps dear old Gloucester here exhausted his taste for wine last night, but I certainly did not.

CORNWALL: Then let's get my lady some wine.

All cheer.

LEAR: Albany.

ALBANY: Yes, Your Majesty.

LEAR: Did you happen to bring me back any of that delicious Spanish wine?

ALBANY: An entire case.

LEAR: Take note, Cornwall: this is how to get on your father-in-law's good side.

All laugh.

GONERIL: Father?

LEAR: Let's have a toast.

Everyone gets a glass and wine.
GONERIL pulls the king aside.

GONERIL: Father?

LEAR: Yes, my dear?

GONERIL: Have you no other announcements to make?

LEAR: Not at this time, my love. Wouldn't want to overshadow your sister's big day.

Beat.

But soon. Soon.

(*a toast*) To the Duke and Duchess of Cornwall!

> *All cheer.*
> *Optimism drains from* GONERIL's *face.*
> *Cool resolve settles in.*
> *An image of* ROZ *from the beginning of the play.*
> *The two exist together.*
> *Blackout.*

Acknowledgements

Thank you to the following artists who contributed to the development of *Queen Goneril*: Damien Atkins, Helen Belay, Kimberly Colburn, Oliver Dennis, Tim Dowler-Coltman, Matthew Edison, Alexis Gordon, Caitie Graham, Virgilia Griffith, Robert Harding, Daren A. Herbert, Lisa Humber, Linda Kash, Breton Lalama, Olivier Lamarche, JD Leslie, Diego Matamoros, Tom McCamus, Patrick McManus, Weyni Mengesha, Natasha Mumba, Nancy Palk, Jordan Pettle, Nadeem Phillip, Sabryn Rock, Kristen Thomson, Amaka Umeh, and Guillermo Verdecchia. *Queen Goneril* was commissioned by Soulpepper Theatre Company's Six Women Writing program with the support of BMO, Project Imagination, and the Women Centre Stage program.

And thank you to Gideon, Olive, and Tallulah for always having my back on this great stage of fools.

Erin Shields is a Canadian playwright based in Toronto. Her adaptation of *Paradise Lost* was commissioned by the Stratford Festival of Canada and won the Quebec Writers Federation Prize for Playwriting. In 2011, Erin won the Governor General's Literary Award for her play *If We Were Birds*, which premiered at Tarragon Theatre. Other theatre credits include *Jane Eyre* (Citadel Theatre), *Piaf/Dietrich* (Mirvish Productions/Segal Centre), *Beautiful Man* (Factory Theatre), *The Lady from the Sea* (The Shaw Festival), *The Millennial Malcontent* and *Soliciting Temptation* (Tarragon Theatre), and *Instant* (Geordie Theatre). For details about upcoming projects see Erin's website, www.erinshields.ca.